DANCING BOYS

High School Males in Dance

The challenges that young women go through in order to be successful in the world of dance are well known. However, little is known about the experiences of young men who choose to take dance classes in non-professional settings.

Dancing Boys is one of the first scholarly works to demystify the largely unknown challenges of adolescent males in dance. Through an ethnographic study of sixty-two adolescent male students, Zihao Li captures the authentic stories and experiences of boys participating in dance classes in a public high school in Toronto. Accompanied by the boys' artwork and photographs and supported by a documentary-style video, the study explores their motivations for dancing, their reflections on masculinity and gender, and the internal and external factors that impact their decisions to continue to dance professionally or in informal settings. With the author's reflections on his own journey as a professional dancer woven throughout, *Dancing Boys* will spark discussion on how educators can, and why they should, engage adolescent males in dance.

ZIHAO LI is an assistant professor in the Faculty of Education at the University of Macau. He has performed with the Guangdong Modern Dance Company, the Hong Kong Dance Company, the City Contemporary Dance Company, and the German Hamburg Ballet.

ZIHAO LI

Dancing Boys

High School Males in Dance

UNIVERSITY OF TORONTO PRESS
Toronto Buffalo London

© University of Toronto Press 2016
Toronto Buffalo London
www.utppublishing.com

ISBN 978-1-4426-4867-8 (cloth)
ISBN 978-1-4426-2632-4 (paper)

Library and Archives Canada Cataloguing in Publication

Li, Zihao, 1975–, author
Dancing boys : high school males in dance / Zihao Li.

Includes bibliographical references and index.
ISBN 978-1-4426-4867-8 (cloth).   ISBN 978-1-4426-2632-4 (paper)

1. Male dancers – Ontario – Toronto – Case studies.   2. High school boys –
Ontario – Toronto – Case studies.   3. Gender identity in dance –
Ontario – Toronto – Case studies.   4. Dance – Social aspects – Ontario –
Toronto – Case studies.   I. Title.

GV1625.5.O7L59 2016   792.80835'1   C2016-902136-X

University of Toronto Press acknowledges the financial assistance to its
publishing program of the Canada Council for the Arts and the Ontario Arts
Council, an agency of the Government of Ontario.

Canada Council
for the Arts

Conseil des Arts
du Canada

ONTARIO ARTS COUNCIL
CONSEIL DES ARTS DE L'ONTARIO

an Ontario government agency
un organisme du gouvernement de l'Ontario

Funded by the
Government
of Canada

Financé par le
gouvernement
du Canada

Canadä

*To my parents, for not giving up on me and not allowing me to give up;
to Maisie, for helping me realize my dream; and to Mary Jane,
for being not only a great teacher but also a friend,
an advisor, and my source of inspiration.*

Contents

List of Illustrations, Figures, and Table   ix

Foreword   xi

Introduction   3

1 I Am a Dancer   9

2 Boys in Dance   22

3 Where Are the Dancing Boys?   40

4 The Voices of the Dancing Boys   55

5 Transformation   75

6 Invisible Barriers   105

7 Dance Experience and Dance Class   120

8 Show Time   137

9 Dancing Through Our Lives   147

Appendix: Video Documentary on Adolescent Male Dance Students   163

References   165

Index   175

Illustrations, Figures, and Table

Illustrations

0.1 Adolescent male students practise in the dance studio 4

1.1 The author (age 18) with other company members and military representatives in southern China 13

1.2 The author (age 11) in front of the Qian Jin Dance Company 13

1.3 The author (age 25) in a poster for the millennium arts celebration 16

1.4 Heather Leslie and the author dance with Desiraeda Dance Theatre 20

3.1 Students from the all-boys class dance in front of Rosedale Heights 42

3.2 A senior dance student from a mixed-gender class dances with an all-boys class 53

4.1 Bruce's visual component, part one: "What Am I Doing?" 59

4.2 Bruce's visual component, part two: "I Am a Man in Ballet" 61

4.3 Michael's visual component: "Getting There" 64

4.4 David's visual component: "I Can Fly" 66

4.5 George's visual component: "Versatility" 68

4.6 Tom's visual component: Untitled (images scanned from his flip book) 70

4.7 Kyle's visual component: "Balance" 73

5.1 Boys interact with each other while backstage 77

5.2 Male dance students pay attention to each other's dance exercises 77

5.3   Two male dance students celebrate their successful "hands-free" lifting   78
5.4   Robert in preschool tap dance   84
7.1   Boys practise split jumps in a ballet class   129
7.2   All-boys dance class students practise their movements in the dance studio   130
7.3   Males in dance classes (mixed-gender and all-boys)   132
7.4   Male dancers practise krumping for the year-end performance   135
8.1   All-boys dance class students practise their year-end performance in the studio   138
8.2   All-boys dance class students practise their year-end performance in the gym   139
8.3   All-boys dance class students perform on the stage   140
8.4   Students from the all-boys dance classes make a "snake pose" during rehearsal   140
8.5   A male student dances "Sleepless Night" on the stage   142
8.6   Dance students warm up in the gym for the year-end dance performance   143
8.7   Adolescent male dance students perform "It's Time" on stage   144
8.8   Adolescent male dance students show off their moves before getting on stage   145

Figures

3.1   Ethnicity of adolescent male dance students   47
3.2   Professions of parents   48
5.1   Reasons to take dance at high school   80
5.2   Preference for male or female dance teachers   88
5.3   Views on dance   95
6.1   Perception of stereotypes in dance   110
6.2   Media and technology's impact on male dance students   116
7.1   Students' future dance plans   124

Table

3.1   The adolescent male dance students studied   44

Foreword

This book by Dr Zihao Li tells two stories: the first concerns a case study of a group of adolescent boys enrolled in a dance class as part of their arts curriculum in secondary school; the second is the author's own narrative of his life as a dancer and dance educator, in Beijing, China, and in Toronto, Canada. These two stories are entwined in this study of why and how and if boys will enter the world of dance, with all of its connotations and historical implications and the gendered, stereotyped, and prejudiced illusions held by those who may have little formal experience with this particular art form.

I have had the pleasure of observing Zihao's professional achievements over several years, both in the school where he taught the boys featured in this book their dance classes and in the arts communities in Toronto where he played a major role in promoting dance education. He blends his own life as a dancer in China with his deep study of the role of dance education in the lives of students to create an unusually integrated philosophy and practice of his chosen discipline. He has worked with students in schools, at universities, and in the professional world, all inside his construct of how dance happens and how dance affects the dancer and the audience.

Dr Li's professional record as a dancer in China and in Canada is outstanding. As well, he has received recognition from a variety of organizations and leading scholars and educators in dance education. They stress his contributions to the field, his impact on dance education programs, his contributions to the growing body of action research, his guidance and support of graduate students, and his role as an advocate for dance pedagogy in educating teachers.

In this book, the reader is caught in the swirl of the arts and humanities education, how participants rethink through action who they are and how their identities are self-altered and discovered as they explore and experiment through the freedom of the arts. Their possibilities unfold as they push through their self-imposed limitations, strengthened and empowered by Zihao's background and knowledge of dance education and by his deep understanding of how students learn through experience and reflection. His case study concerns the boys in one class, and he captures their journeys into his educational world, from their hesitant beginnings to their confident public sharing of what they have learned. Zihao is always alongside their involvement, and in doing so he continues to shift his own understanding of the students and to recognize their place in their own learning curves so he can offer them possibilities through their practice as they tap into imaginative and creative responses.

Zihao has examined the literature on boys and dance, and his insights offer us ways of reconsidering our own perceptions of why and how boys choose dance instruction, helping us to examine our gendered construction of males who choose to dance. As the "boy code" morphs into new reinterpretations of masculine identity, we can actually hear the very changes we hope for in the boys' words in this book, their different reasons for entering into the world of dance, and their struggles for recognition and affirmation from their male peers, the girls in their social groups, their families, and their teachers. Their experiences of dancing in school provide us with useful information as we confront and challenge notions of "being a boy" in the culture of school.

I want to note especially Zihao's commitment to his art form, to excellence in dance, to quality instruction and technique. He is a person of great integrity, and his insight into the professions of dance and of teaching is remarkable. He blends and integrates both and represents the artist/teacher/academic as few are able to do. I value him as a colleague, as a researcher, as a professional dancer, as a teacher, and as a model for young people entering the arts world.

The dance is in Zihao Li, and he dances. And the boys in his class, they dance. And we who believe in the arts in education for all, we celebrate with them.

David Booth
University of Toronto
2015

DANCING BOYS

High School Males in Dance

Introduction

With the rise of popular TV programs such as *Dancing with the Stars* and *So You Think You Can Dance* and films including *Rize* (2005) and *Save the Last Dance* (2001), it would seem that males in dance are absolutely normal and legitimate. It is not uncommon to see plenty of males performing ethnic and cultural dances (particularly Latinos and African Americans), in professional dance shows, dances related to religious ceremonies (First Nations traditional dances, Tibetan rituals), and other popular social dance forms (hip hop, krump, pop, and now Gangnam style). Many males would see the intrinsic and extrinsic values of dance but they would not pursue dance as a career. That leads to an embarrassing situation in that there are hardly any males in dance classes. The lack of males in dance is particularly severe in public schools, dance studios, and college/university dance programs.

Where are the male dancers, especially adolescent males, when we look at dance classes held in conventional dance training venues such as dance studios and high schools? That is still a common question which puzzles many dance educators, who are currently facing an extreme ratio imbalance between male and female dance students. By focusing on the experiences of a few adolescent male dance students who choose to venture into dance during their public high school years, this book investigates and explores the largely unknown realities of adolescent males taking dance in high school, regarding what they have gone through before, during, and after taking dance. This study takes place at Rosedale Heights School of the Arts in Toronto (Illus. 0.1). Unlike most other arts schools, Rosedale Heights does not require students to audition to be admitted to the school (Toronto District School Board [TDSB], 2009b). Dance is offered as an optional course that all students are welcome to take regardless

Illus. 0.1. Adolescent male students practise in the dance studio
at Rosedale Heights[1]

of their skill level or background. More about the school is discussed in
chapter 2, "Boys in Dance." This is a book about practice, dance practice,
and boys in dance practice. This volume pays tribute to adolescent male
students who challenge the dominant perceptions of masculinity by participating in dance at a public high school in Toronto, Canada.

Critical dance studies focusing on masculinity have appeared since the
1990s. Ramsay Burt "examines the representation of masculinity in twentieth century dance" in *The Male Dancer: Bodies, Spectacle, Sexualities* (Burt,
1995) and in *Alien Bodies: Representations of Modernity, "Race," and Nation
in Early Modern Dance* (Burt, 1998). His books focus on prejudices against
male dancers and also look at established male dancers through race,
class, culture, and geographical location. Michael Gard (2006) investigates "how the worlds of Western theatrical dance, gender relations and
sexuality intermingle" in *Men Who Dance: Aesthetics, Athletics and the Art of*

---

1 All images are credited to the author unless otherwise noted.

Masculinity. He talks extensively about socially constructed theories behind males' reluctance to participate in dance. Although these studies make an important contribution to our understanding of the male dancer, no one has focused extensively on the adolescent male dancer beginning dance. This book centres on practice by looking at high school males who take part in dance. This book is about my life and the lives of the boys I research. This book is about dancing boys; I am one of them.

Before I start, I would like to define some terms. "Formal" points to professional dance training programs, "informal" talks about recreational/educational dance classes, and "pre-professional" refers to training institutions that prepare individuals for a dance career. Note that both formal and pre-professional groups include male dancers/students who started with informal dance training. Almost all male dancers with whom I have worked admitted that they started dancing as an interest before turning it into a career. Many critical dance theories focus on the formal and pre-professional groups that often display no gender imbalance issues. Males and females are already auditioned and selected by this stage. My study instead looks at the informal group, from which most professional and pre-professional dancers developed. In reality, younger males can rarely be found taking dance in informal dance training facilities (studios, public and private schools, and community centres). Studies focusing on young male dancers are scarce but much needed, not only for educational and scholarly reasons but also for reasons of equity. Adolescence is a formative age for developing the skills and attitudes required to consider a professional career in dance. Reputable male dancers such as José Limón,[2] Paul Taylor,[3] and Alvin Ailey[4] started dancing in their late adolescent years, and all became hugely successful figures in American modern dance.

At the Hong Kong Academy for Performing Arts, where I received my bachelor of fine arts degree, ballet instructors constantly faced a dilemma

---

2 José Limón (1908–72) is considered one of the pioneers in modern dance and choreography of the twentieth century. His works have influenced many audiences and are still performed today by his company and others.

3 Paul Taylor is one of the modern dance pioneers in the United States. He performed in the companies of Merce Cunningham, Martha Graham, and George Balanchine, and founded his own company, the Paul Taylor Dance Company, in 1954.

4 Alvin Ailey (1931–89) was one of the most influential modern dance choreographers in the world. He founded the first all-black dance company, the Alvin Ailey American Dance Theater in the United States.

when teaching the partnering class because of the lack of male ballet dancers and the much larger female population. It became such a problem that the dean of dance encouraged – perhaps pressured – all male dance students to take the partnering class, even when they were concentrating in modern or Chinese dance studies. The academy even offered scholarships to foreign male dance students such as myself to fill the gap. Many years later, when I taught first-year ballet and modern dance classes at York University in Canada, there were 68 dance students, but only 4 were males; one of them was an exchange student from England and another dropped out of university in the middle of the first semester. After two months, there were 66 girls and 2 boys, similar to the situation in Hong Kong. While teaching with the Toronto District School Board, I happened to be the only full-time male dance teacher in the entire school board, which employs over 36,500 teachers in nearly 600 schools (TDSB, 2016).

In Western countries, modern and ballet are taught in the majority of dance institutions from amateur to professional levels. Most dance educators themselves have had modern and ballet training prior to their teaching career. There are many teaching resources with regard to the instruction, assessment, and evaluation for modern and ballet. However, adolescent males seem to be more interested in popular dance forms such as hip hop and krump,[5] as can be seen by the number of popular dance groups as extracurricular activities and school clubs. In consideration of this, one reason for the low numbers of males in dance classes may be systemic discrimination in the way the dance curriculum is being delivered.

This book is not a novel endeavour, since there is a significant amount of research on adult males in dance and established male dancers through academic and popular culture lenses (Burt, 1995; Desmond, 2001; Gard, 2001; Gard, 2006; Gard, 2008; Keyworth, 2001; Risner, 2008; Risner, 2009a; Risner, 2009b; Risner, 2009c). Those studies often focus on established male dancers – what they have achieved and accomplished in and around dance. The closest one to this study is Risner's (2009c) *Stigma and Perseverance in the Lives of Boys Who Dance: An Empirical Study of Male Identities in Western Theatrical Dance Training*, in which he looks at males (aged 13–22) who are actively involved in pre-professional dance training

---

5 Krump is a form of street dance. It is popular in many Western countries including the United States and England. Krump is recognized by its percussive, individualistic, and energetic movement involving all body parts.

institutions. Risner's two-phase, three-year study of 75 male participants provides invaluable scholarship on the topic. He concludes, "While some cultures see dance as a valid career option, dominant Western paradigm positions concert dance as a predominantly 'female' activity and art form" (p. 2). Nonetheless, Gard (2008) comments that research on males (regardless of their age and who they are) about why they dance and how they think and feel when they dance remains extremely inadequate. Overall, academic resources (ERIC, Scholars Portal, JSTOR, and Pro-Quest) and public domains (public libraries and bookstores) show limited results for in-depth research on boys of post-primary-school age who dance and on pre-professional-level male dancers (ages 13 to 18). Scholar Jane Desmond (1993) stated, "Dance remains a greatly undervalued and under theorized arena of bodily discourse" (p. 35). A few existing books examine male dancers either from the physical education perspective or from the perspective of established male dancers. Although these professional dancers are possible role models for young boys to follow, adolescent males continue to be few in number in regular dance classes. The gap between the fame of those successful male dancers and the challenges that adolescent males face in dance on a day-to-day basis seems to be too big to cross without some support.

As a first step to bridging this gap, I begin my investigation in a public high school setting where dance is offered as an elective course. With an array of means – autobiography, interviews, videotape, and performance – I investigate and explore the largely unknown realities regarding adolescent male dance students: why they decide to take dance; the influence of other factors (family, friends, siblings) on their decision to take dance; what makes them continue or stop dancing; how their perceptions of dance are transformed over time; their views of different dance classes; how they feel when they are dancing; the realities they embody in studio and on stage; their message to the public about who they were, who they are, and what they want to be in and through dance; the effect of the gender of the dance teacher; the impact from multimedia (Internet, YouTube) and TV shows (e.g., *So You Think You Can Dance, Dancing with the Stars*); and the star/idol effect (e.g., Alvin Ailey, Mikhail Baryshnikov, Gene Kelly).

The evidence collected challenges the socially constructed epistemology that dance, regardless of form, is a less legitimate subject of study than traditional subjects. It reminds us of the crucial relationship between mind and body and also brings to the surface various issues including ethnic background, identity, physical education and dance, the professional and the novice, female and male dance educators, dance pedagogy (theory) and curriculum delivery (practice), and the association of homosexuality and heterosexuality in the context of dance and its effect on adolescent male students' willingness to dance.

The information in this book on adolescent males in dance will benefit teachers, dance instructors, curriculum theorists, professors, and even professional dancers and choreographers in terms of understanding young male dancers – their needs, fears, attitudes, and expectations. I acknowledge that the context of this study is limited. Nevertheless, my hope is that this study is a first step and will generate more discussion, spark more interest, and result in more research about adolescent males in dance. Writing this book certainly helped me understand my own personal journey from an average boy to a dance student, to a professional dancer, and now to a dancer, dance teacher, and a researcher. I sincerely hope that we, as educators, will be able to use these findings to promote dance among adolescent males and to find strategies to keep them in dance.

British novelist Jeanette Winterson (1995) asserts that combining autobiography and self-reflection is probably the best way to understand ourselves as narratives on a larger scale, to know who we are and what we can become. Unveiling my dance experience in the past has helped me to better understand the struggles I have gone through as a male dancer, and in turn, I am better able to make sense of the autobiographical writings of the students presented in chapter 4. I find it intriguing that our experiences share so many similarities even though they have occurred in a different context, time, place, and culture. In my case, I have gone through strict and disciplined dance training and have continued to dance professionally, whereas these young males have taken dance as an optional course in a public high school, some merely out of curiosity. Griffin (1995) writes, "We live in the present time, where the past and future are tangled and intertwined lines composing and creating who we are today" (p. 149). It is the boys' stories and mine together, both present and past, that may create a better understanding of adolescent male dancers.

1

I Am a Dancer

To achieve some depth in your field requires a lot of sacrifices. Want to or not, you're thinking about what you're doing in life – in my case, dancing. Dancing is my obsession. My life.

Mikhail Baryshnikov

I am sitting on a plane en route to Hong Kong, then Macau, to take up a university teaching position. With my eyes closed, my thoughts have never settled peacefully. As a male thriving in a female-dominated profession, I have never completely stopped doubting my choice or my parents' decision to encourage me to become a dancer, then a teacher, and now a university professor. Six hours into the 15-hour flight, many passengers have fallen sleep. For the first time in my life I am not travelling alone but accompanied by Maisie, my wife; Wendy, my mother-in-law; Isaac, my five-year-old son; and Sophie, my daughter, who just turned two. This is not one of my regular trips to present a research paper, teach some master classes, or attend yet another dance conference. In 10 hours, my entire family plus 12 suitcases will arrive in Macau, where I will be teaching Sixteenth-Century French Court dance at the University of Macau. Anxious, scared, and worried, I am stepping into a new world that is far too similar and yet different. A world that is filled with the unknown, excitement, and challenge, and I will be dancing in it. I am a male dancer and dancing is part of my life.

Thirty Years Ago, the Mid-1980s

Like many adolescent males in dance, my path was not a smooth one. I lived in a time when breakdance and the Jackson Five ruled popular culture. As a young boy training as a dancer in northern China, I was hugely affected by Western culture. My friends and I tried to do moon-walks and head spins until we saw the movie *White Nights*, which featured Mikhail Baryshnikov's legendary tale of escaping from Russia to the United States. Baryshnikov's incredible jumps and turns not only wowed me but also opened my eyes to a different world of dance.

I grew up with girls, many girls – dancing, rehearsing, performing, and putting on make-up. As a result, I often heard comments like "you are so lucky that you dance with girls" or "you must love dancing dearly." I smiled each time but seldom responded because I knew that my answer might not make any sense to them. In fact, becoming a dancer was one of the toughest decisions that I had ever made in my life. Dancing did not become my obsession, nor my life, until much later.

A Glimpse into My Past

Pre-dance Training

I did not want to dance. I hated being one of the only boys dancing with more than 40 girls. I did not know why but I felt embarrassed, uncom-fortable, and sometimes even a bit humiliated during dance class. As a young boy, I did not even know that there was such a profession for males. I thought dance was for girls and weaker people, those who always cried, even though back then, I did cry quite a lot.

I was born in Harbin, a city in the northeast of China with a population of 10 million people – small compared to Beijing and Shanghai.[1] Because I was born into a typical family with no one involved in the arts, my family never thought that I would become a professional male dancer. My father was a policeman and my mother worked in a school kitchen.

When I was five years old, my father enrolled me in dance without even asking me. Like many boys, I did not like dancing. My father wanted me to have something different from other children, an edge, perhaps a skill that would help me get somewhere. According to a conversation we had years later, he confessed that he thought if nothing resulted from my dance training, at least I would end up with a good body, or to be more accurate, a healthy body.

---

1 Compared with other big cities such as Beijing (21 million) and Shanghai (24 million), Harbin is a mid- to small-scale city in China. China's population is 1.3 billion.

I enjoyed the exhilarating jumps and skips that boys get to do in dance. We got to jump higher and skip farther than the girls. Even the accompanist (usually a pianist) played a slower tempo to suit our grand movements. Unfortunately, that was only a small portion of the entire dance class. For the most part, I had to dance with girls, and there were many of them.

One memorable experience stemmed from the shocking disparity between boys and girls. There were approximately 40 students in the class and I was one of two boys. Being a minority in class, boys often had to learn girls' dance steps. We found it objectionable and yet there was nothing we could do. The dance teacher was too busy with the girls, and he rarely even had time to notice that there were boys in his class. There was no relevant curriculum designed for boys in dance training at the time. At a young age (seven), I had already made up my mind that one day I would create a dance class that would make boys want to dance and let them feel proud of themselves while dancing.

Dance Training

In those days, parents were actually allowed to sit in the dance studio to watch their children dancing. We had a class of 40 to 50 dance students and there were often as many parents in the studio, if not more. To my parents, weather and even sickness were not legitimate reasons for me not to go to dance classes. Although I became good at dancing before I left the school, I still did not like it because there were too many girls. None of my male classmates from day school took dance. I felt that I was doing something embarrassing or even sinful. As a result, I seldom told others, especially my friends in school, about my involvement in dance. I remember that I used to ask my aunt to bring my ballet slippers to the dance studio because I did not want my friends to see that I had them, let alone that I actually wore them. Even at the end of my training when I was considered a senior student (age 11), I felt uncomfortable whenever I was asked to present something in front of the class. One instance stands out clearly.

I was about 10 years old at the time. My teacher asked me to go to the front of the class and do a handstand, with both hands supporting the whole body upside down. I had done handstands many times before, but this time was different. The teacher did not let me down immediately. Instead, he held my feet and started talking about how to point the feet and hold the back straight. This handstand became strenuous and my body started to sink; I could hear other children laughing. My heart sank to the lowest point since I had started dancing. Any good memories of dancing were erased instantly by that traumatic experience. I continued my dance training in that studio until I was 11 years old. Then, Qian Jin Dance Company came to Harbin to audition potential dance trainees – 10 boys and 10 girls, ages 10 or 11 only. I knew in my heart that this audition was my only opportunity to get out of my hometown dance studio. My goal was to get through and be selected. I went to the audition, along with a few thousand others. It was a gruelling audition that involved many stages held in different cities. Examiners scrutinized us in detail: from basic physical measurement (longer legs than arms, slim body structure) to being able to learn intricate choreographies. At the final stage, we were asked to perform a dance in front of an audience in the company headquarters, Shenyang, a city 600 kilometres from my hometown. The entire auditioning process took three months, during which I saw my friends, including my only male classmate, get eliminated. My parents were thrilled when they learned that I was selected. I was confused because I did not do anything special, and I was scared because I did not know how my future would unfold.

I became injured during the audition process, and when a school classmate asked me why I was limping, my response was that I fell. I still did not want others to know that I was in dance. After I was chosen, my regular school teacher, upon hearing the news, announced to the class, "Classmate Li is accepted by the Qian Jin Dance Company and he will become a captain in the army. We wish him the best and we look forward to seeing him in a military uniform in the future." I could not help but notice that she did not say, "He will study dance and become a professional dancer." I could feel my face burning.

The Qian Jin Dance Company was an organization affiliated with the People's Liberation Army (PLA). The Chinese military force was so huge in number, close to five million in the 1980s, that it had its own hospitals, factories, farms, and even entertainment groups (dance, drama, acrobatic, and opera). The Chinese government, led by its Communist Party members, valued the arts (visual arts, music, drama, and dance) and hence invested financially in these troupes to "support" its large military needs (Illus. 1.1). Little did I know at the time that professional dance training was far more gruesome than what I had previously experienced. I had to work hard, not necessarily to become the best dancer but simply to continue in the company. When others went to bed, I went to the dance studio to practise what we had learned during the day. All staff including singers, dancers, and visual arts designers in the company wore military uniforms, something I had desired since I was little (Illus. 1.2).

Illus. 1.1. The author (age 18), second row far right, in costume with other company members and military representatives in southern China

Illus. 1.2. The author (age 11) standing in front of the Qian Jin Dance Company's building

Although it was seen as a privilege to be in the army as a dancer, I still was not convinced that I wanted to continue to dance.

As dance students, we were trained in classical ballet by Russian Vaganova[2] experts and later by Chinese military dance masters after the relationship between China and Russia deteriorated. When we danced on stage, our movements were usually modified in a way to look like Chinese dance. For instance, our legs would be parallel or even turned in rather than turned out while turning or posing on balance. Depending on our role on stage, we would either wear military uniforms or hold the Communist Party flag while dancing. At one point, one of us questioned the purpose of classical ballet in training. Our choreographers and dance masters replied that classical ballet was a means to make us strong dancers. After six years of training in the company as a trainee and an apprentice, I secured a precious tenured contract position while one-third of the original group of dance students was eliminated during the training process. Nonetheless, deep down in my heart, I was still not completely convinced that professional dancing was my calling.

While training with the company, I did not have to pay for anything. Tuition, food, clothing, transportation, and accommodation were all covered. We even received a little allowance each month. Even with all of these advantages, I doubted whether I should continue dancing. From time to time during those teenage years, I thought that males, including myself, should not be in dance; rather, they should pursue careers that seemed to be more "macho" or "manly." My self-doubt lingered even after I was promoted to the rank of captain and received benefits and pay comparable to my father's after he had worked 15 years in the police force. I was also selected to join the PLA's core party – the Communist Party of China. At the age of 20, I was given sleek military uniforms and made more money than my parents combined. I was in a strange situation. On the one hand, I was admired by many others. On the other hand, I wanted to be out.

As a professional dancer, I did what I had to do to dance well and show others that I deserved what I had. With that mentality, training both physically and mentally, I went on to dance professionally for many years with different companies – Guangdong Modern Dance Company, Germany's Hamburg Ballet, Hong Kong City Contemporary Dance Company, Hong

---

2 Vaganova is a form of ballet technique and one of the major training methods developed by the Russian dancer and pedagogue Agrippina Vaganova (1879–1951).

Kong Dance Company, Toronto's Desiraeda Dance Theatre, and most recently Opera Atelier in Toronto. On various dance scholarships, I was able to complete a BFA and an MA degree in dance and recently a doctorate in education. While studying at the Hong Kong Academy for the Performing Arts, I received an American Dance Festival scholarship that was so lucrative it covered everything including my tuition, accommodation, meals, and even bus fare throughout my university stay in Hong Kong, one of the most expensive cities in the world. I proved myself when an image of me dancing was featured on posters all over Hong Kong for the millennium arts celebration (Illus. 1.3).

Nonetheless, there were still many challenges for me to stay in dance. I was not alone: my parents told me that even they thought at times that dance was not the best choice for me. On numerous occasions, I found myself asking, "Who am I?" and "What am I doing?" I continued in this profession in spite of the questions I had about my own identity and self-worth in dance. Should I have believed my reviews?

"After ferocious competition, Zihao is the finalist to receive the prestigious scholarship from the American Dance Festival to study at the Hong Kong Academy for Performing Arts." Zhao (1997), *Guangzhou Daily*

"Zihao Li is a rising star in dance community …" Ou (1995), *Beijing Youth Daily*

"His dance touches every single audience's heart, etc. … Li Zihao is, undoubtedly, the millennium dancer of the year." Hua (2000), *Singtao Daily*

"Zihao's dancing moved the people of Prague, Czech Republic." Yue (2000), *Da Gong Daily*

"Zihao is on the wall of fame at this year's international dance festival." Citron (2005a), *Globe and Mail*

"Zihao is a sensational dancer with superb ballet technique." Citron (2005b), *Globe and Mail*[3]

---

3 These newspaper articles and reviews about me as a dancer were published between 1995 and 2006.

Illus. 1.3. The author (age 25) featured in a poster for the millennium
arts celebration in Hong Kong. Courtesy of Hong Kong Academy
for Performing Arts/香港演藝學院

One intriguing discovery I made was that when I performed on stage, this feeling of bewilderment disappeared. I wrote the following poem to capture some of the internal dialogue I had while dancing.

Plié
Turn out
Stand up
Breathe
Don't give up

Bend your knees!
Chin up
Head up
Back straight

Don't give up

Stretch
Stretch further! Harder!
Stretch till it almost breaks
Stretch!!!

Don't give up

I breathe
I pirouette
I stumble
I fall, I get up, and I try it again

Don't give up

It's painful
It's tiring
It's hard
It makes me feel good

I am not giving up

While I dance
I am myself

I am on fire
I know that I am fully in charge

I am not giving up

In dance
My mind and body merge
My imagination explodes
My expression expands
I will never give up
I am a dancer – a male dancer

Zihao Li, November 2008

It took me years to consolidate my thoughts into a clear understanding of who I am. However, if I could restart my life, I might not gone into dance or stayed in this profession for this long. It was not something that I wanted to do in the first place but something I accidentally stumbled upon. Socially constructed meanings and definitions of gender have prevented many males from getting into dance. When I was a young boy in northern China, I had a broad and vague understanding of masculinity and what males are supposed to do and not do. Friends, classmates, and family members around me never told me not to dance, but somehow in the way they looked at me or talked about my decision to dance they seemed to be amused rather than appreciative of my special talent. It seemed that their responses and compliments were not as sincere and honest as I expected. Why were they laughing when they heard that I studied dance? Why were they shocked? Why did they say, "Wow, dance! Seriously?" Perhaps it was my own feeling of insecurity or perhaps I was overly sensitive. I asked the young males in this study similar questions and found there were more similarities than differences. Many adolescent males taking dance in this particular arts school also experienced self-doubt and feeling marginalized, as I had when I was young. The context was different, as I was chosen to be trained in an elite group where option and choice were non-existent. The majority of adolescent males in this study made their own decision to take dance in high school. Many of them continued to take dance for a number of years, and several even became professional dancers. I grew up in a much more controlled and restricted environment – old China, where authority (parents and teachers) was unquestionable. Young boys in this study enjoyed much-desired freedom and rights in a modern and well-developed country – Canada. Why were our initial thoughts on dance so similar? Thirty years later, the majority of my professionally trained classmates are no longer dancing. Neither are many boys in this study, as many of them stopped training after high school. Despite our geographic, socio-economic, time, and cultural differences, the outcome was surprisingly similar. Was that just coincidence? Did all boys experience the feeling of being marginalized when they started dancing? What happened to those boys who did not possess any negative feelings about taking dance? What made them immune from the negativity and how did they feel while dancing? On the other hand, what could we, dance educators and curriculum/policy writers, do to ease other young males' initial stress about taking dance? With all these questions in mind, I hope that this book provides some answers with which we can better understand young males in dance.

Thirty Years Later, 2014

Time flies. Looking back, I can hardly imagine how I endured those gruelling years. Yet dance has played a critical role in shaping my life. Through dance I have been transformed; I have accomplished more than I could ever imagine. And still I have more than once contemplated quitting dance in the last 25 years. The fact is that there are many explicit and implicit obstacles that keep males from participating in dance. Twyla Tharp, an Emmy Award winner, describes male dancers as a rare breed. Some take dance at a preschool age but quit soon after, thinking of dance as an activity for girls. Even now, I have more acquaintances who are women than men because of my profession.

As I look back and analyse my autobiography, I can more readily see the obstacles that hindered my growth as an adolescent dancer and the influences that helped me to continue. These insights and experiences have served as tools for me to "unearth the voices" of the young male dancers in this book. They also provide me with different lenses to see their experiences while taking dance.

One of the insights I have used is my experience with "optimal flow." Csikszentmihalyi (1990) describes optimal flow as a state of being totally absorbed in a task, hence allowing the individual to perform at optimal levels. While dancing, I know that I am truly myself. I am in control by being completely involved in the interaction with spectators through physical movements and meaning making (meanings and messages embodied within those movements). Time seems to be suspended and I know that what I am doing is meaningful, powerful, and worthwhile (Illus. 1.4).

Illus. 1.4. Heather Leslie and the author dance with Desiraeda
Dance Theatre at the Toronto Fringe Festival (2008)
Photo by Ryan Faubert

Another insight is the moment of self-realization. The dance experience creates a cycle of reward, which drives me to do better and to continue in dance. To me, dance is intrinsically rewarding, and it brings a sense of jubilation that makes me want to dance. This intrinsic reward, the moment of self-realization, can later be reinforced extrinsically by public recognition.

Not only have these insights helped me recognize instances of optimal flow and self-realization in the boys' stories, but I have also used these insights as tools to frame questions to learn why these adolescent boys have stayed in dance. Hopefully, the findings in this book will be helpful for other adolescent male students contemplating dance, and perhaps even other male dancers more broadly who are struggling with their identity, facing peer pressures, or wrestling with family members' approval to participate in dance.

2

Boys in Dance

Dance and I became inseparable at an early stage of my life. At age 11, I was among the finalists (10 boys and 10 girls, all 10 and 11 years old) in the Qian Jin Dance Company. We were considered the lucky ones as thousands had been shut out over numerous rounds of auditions and interviews. As young dance students, we looked almost identical thanks to the strict selection process: long legs, short upper body, clean-cut hairstyle. During all classes, the boys were required to wear no more than tiny shorts and a tank top, and the girls were in bodysuits. We lived in a big dorm room, where our bedding, blankets, and even school bags were exactly the same (all supplies were distributed by the central office). We boys dressed differently from the girls, yet we had a narrow understanding of what masculine meant. Even more troublesome, we often had difficulty explaining dance to some of our family members and friends, especially those who were not closely related to us. During the 10 years I stayed in the company, I had little knowledge of what was going on outside the dance world because of our busy training schedule and the pressure to cling to our precious spot (if anyone showed any kind of weakness in either technique or emotion, he or she would be sent home immediately). Boys in this study, on the other hand, had full access to the outside world. They had all the privileges that other adolescents enjoyed: freedom, shopping, the Internet, and Facebook, among others. Were they better informed about masculinity and gender, so they took dance? Not necessarily. Many adolescent males in this study did not give a clear definition of what masculinity was, but they did admit that advancement of technology and the Internet affected their way of thinking about dance for males. In some cases, they took dance because they had seen it online or watched it on popular television programs, such as *So You Think You*

Can Dance. Technology and popular media, in some ways, legitimized their action of taking dance.

When I was a young dancer in China, more than two decades ago, very few people spoke about masculinity and even fewer talked about sexuality. The latter was a "taboo" topic, as the majority of people including myself had little or no knowledge of gay, lesbian, bisexual, and transsexual issues. In the 1990s, China was undergoing a drastic change, which was arguably propelled by the Tiananmen Square student movement in 1989. Western art such as impressionist and postmodern artworks and music, modern dance, theatre, and popular movies slowly found its way into China. Perhaps the speed of change was too fast; many people, myself included, found it hard to balance the traditional values and new thinking. I found myself becoming more dependent on dance because it made me focus on what I was supposed to do. It was then that dance started to become my salvation, although lots of doubts remained with me for many more years.

Dance played an important role in helping me define masculinity in narrow terms. Dance was clearly classified between male and female roles: the way we moved, paused, showed our facial expressions. We were trained in Chinese classical dance and ballet; male teachers taught males and female teachers trained females. Ballet teachers from Russia (then Soviet Union) showed us dance videos of George Balanchine, Mikhail Baryshnikov, and Rudolf Nureyev. They emphasized that manly dancing was jumping high and executing multiple turns. These teachers made masculinity quite easy to understand from a dance perspective. Nonetheless, I felt embarrassed for being called a "dancing boy" when I went back home to visit family and friends in the summer and during the Chinese New Year. On those occasions the meaning of dance was not relevant to those who were not in dance. I was the only person involved in dance in my family, and I could not relate to male relatives and friends, who were pursuing more manly careers. Similar findings were also identified through this study even though the experiences were two decades apart and the dancers lived on different continents. Interviews with boys at Rosedale Heights School of the Arts in Toronto revealed that the majority of boys had made up their own mind to take dance. However, most of these boys were reluctant to speak about dance in public. Their unwillingness to speak about dance intensified when they socialized with people with whom they were not familiar. Some boys in this study admitted that they had experienced misunderstandings outside of school and that they were afraid of being bullied because of their participation in dance.

It was evident that a particular school environment – or, in my case, a dance company – creates a much more welcoming place for boys to participate in and talk about dance. In places outside of that environment, it was still challenging for males to speak about dance. It was even harder to talk about gender and masculinity in dance because of our limited knowledge about both.

Redefining Gender and Masculinity through Dance

To many, gender is simply ticking a box labelled "male" or "female." Social scientists differentiate gender as the "manner in which culture defines and constrains these differences in the manner in which individuals view both themselves and others, in terms of the female/male dichotomy" (Siann, 2013, p. 3). In dance, the ideas of gender are not as clear: what are the gender issues in dance? Who should be taking dance? Are dancing boys gay? If they are gay, are they still considered masculine males? How do straight boys see themselves in dance? How do they respond to unpleasant comments, feelings, and views on males in dance? These are difficult questions to answer and we have to look to the research for a better understanding.

Hargreaves and Anderson (2014) state that "gender is a very complex and changing social category of analysis both in relation to the opposite sex and within one's sexual category" (p. 3). Socially constructed interpretations of gender have produced dominant ideas of males and females; masculinity and femininity. These interpretations have a major impact on our lives with respect to how we see and understand what is considered a masculine career. Given that dance is represented mostly by females in Western countries, many males would not consider dance a manly career. This study confirms that finding but argues that when males actually participated in dance for a certain period of time, their views on dance changed. Gallagher (2006) also raises a series of questions in this regard, looking at this matter through "interrelated lenses of race, class, sexuality, disability, ethnicity, accent discrimination, and sexism." She further suggests that educators must examine in their practice and research the ways in which sexuality and other identity markers are socially constructed and performed, how the moral, gendered, and discoursed cultures created in classrooms reinscribe historical inequities (p. 71).

To many, gender is socially ascribed at birth, along with all the binary expressions that a culture will condone. The male dancing body, in contrast, is perceived as emotional, eroticized, and perhaps sexualized by others, in a way that is generally not permitted for males. In my case, the uncomfortable and even shameful feelings about being a male dancer, mixed with the unexplained thrill and happiness I experienced from dancing on stage, created paradoxical emotions in my early dancing career.

Twenty years later when I began this study, I was fascinated to discover that adolescent males faced similar struggles in a completely different place, time, and culture. While the boys chose dance for different reasons (healthy living style, physical activity, fun, etc.), dance was still a sexualized subject, which formed barriers between them and other boys. In recent years, however, notably in the West, a rapidly growing recognition of sexual diversity and greater tolerance of homosexuality have led to a lessening of homophobia (Anderson, 2010) and bisexual phobia (Ripley, Anderson, McCormack, and Rockett, 2012). The concept of male dancers started to change, both for male dancers themselves and for others. Popular culture, media, and technology were contributors to this evolving process.

Booth (2002) asserted, "What it means to be a boy or a girl in school is to a large degree dependent upon the school's culture or the classroom's subculture" (p. 13). As adolescent male dancers in the 1980s, we were not able to talk about the meanings of masculinity and sexuality, nor were we interested in exploring further. We were curious, but there was nobody to help us understand. Years later, I learned that masculinity and sexuality were socially constructed and how they were experienced and defined depended on individual social networks (Booth, 2002, p. 14).

Male Dancers' Identity

Research studies suggest that men who enter female-dominated professions are often identified as "failures or sexual deviants" even though they tend to rise to higher managerial positions and receive higher pay, despite intense female competition. Men are also favoured as role models in the sense that they have more chances to climb the job ladder (Acker, 1994; Gard, 2008; Williams, 1995). Overall, male dancers have more opportunities to be promoted to a higher position even though they face more female competitors in the field. One wonders why males still opt to stay away from dance despite the opportunity of achieving such power. Perhaps it is because adolescent males formulate their gender identity through social interactions with others (especially with similar age-group peers). Curriculum theorist Dewey (2007) describes the creation of an individual's sense of belonging in his book *Experience and Education*:

> The extension in space of the number of individuals who participate in an interest so that each has to refer his own action to that of others, and to consider the action of others to give point and direction to his own, is equivalent to the breaking down of those barriers of class, race, and national territory which kept men from perceiving the full import of their activity. (p. 83)

A similar argument is presented by Lorber (1994), as she asserts,

> Most people, however, voluntarily go along with their society's prescriptions for those of their gender status because the norms and expectations get built into their sense of worth and identity as a certain kind of human being and because they believe their society's way is the natural way. (p. 129)

Researchers at the University of Newcastle in Australia have found that dance is presented as a feminine domain and boys are turned off by the dance experiences they have had early in life, mainly in primary school (Bev, 2001). Lipscomb (1986) suggests that "boys struggle from their initial dance experiences, if any, which mostly focus on creative and improvisatory approaches," such as being told to make tableaux, to be trees, or to express their feeling through shapes (p. 65). At first, this may seem like a gross generalization, but it is evident that the negative experience at the beginning stage does exist, as shown by most of the interviews in this study. Perhaps that initial struggle was a result of lack of dance experience earlier in their life. The fact is that females outnumber males both as students and teachers in many school-based dance programs and regular dance studios. It is not uncommon for males to follow/learn female steps in dance classes because there are many more females, which is one of the struggles males face while taking dance. A number of researchers suggest reasons for this struggle. Berger (2003) argues that the lack of respect given to the position of male dancers, which requires a substantial amount of strength and skill, has created such "gender impositions" in dance. Williams (1995) further suggests that "all forms of masculinity have one characteristic in common: the imperative of being different from and superior to femininity" (p. 120). In this context, that difference refers to the fact that males should not do something (dance) that females like to do. In a North American setting, when boys reach school age, the majority realize that dance is probably not a "manly" activity since most of their peers are involved in hockey and baseball. Although they may have had positive dance experiences, boys at this age usually make the switch away from dance to avoid being discriminated against or even harassed. Many young males begin to perceive dance as homosexual and sports as heterosexual. They are not alone, as Gard (2003a) asserts that public displays of men participating in dance are seen as "unambiguously (homo)sexual and therefore immoral" (p. 215); Adler (2002) reiterates that boys who are not considered to be successful athletes are, unfortunately, labelled "gay" in high school (p. 202); Griffin (1995) states that "sports prowess" is a means for males to show others and themselves that they are heterosexual; and Risner (2009b) directly points out that "dance is viewed as a feminine activity, all males who dance (whether gay or straight) are always in danger of being classified as effeminate, girly, not 'real men'" (p. 1).

American modern dance pioneer Ted Shawn[1] noticed this discrepancy in gender representation in dance more than 100 years ago. His way of fighting the problem was to create an all-male dance company and to exaggerate "masculinity" by exhibiting muscular and athletic males dancing on stage (Foulkes, 2001). In his time, sports were constructed as a completely heterosexual male practice. As masculinity researchers try to comprehend the past, Shawn reminds us that both sports and dance remain discursive as well as material. Sports and dance construct and occupy significant if evolving places within the project of gender identity construction, particularly for boys and men, and the perpetuation of heterosexual male power. Many males choose sports as one of the means through which they can justify their heterosexual identity and claim their masculinity (Connell, 1995; Kidd, 1987; Martino, 1999; Messner, 1999). The widespread images and televised events such as the Super Bowl and National Hockey League games certainly promote such "man + sports = muscular/heterosexual" attitude.

Risner (2008) discusses in depth the social stigma attached to males who dance. Lever (1978) and Scraton (1986) suggest that boys prefer sports and girls prefer dance partially because of the conflicts of "values"

---

1 Ted Shawn has been referred to as the father of American dance. He co-established with Ruth St Denis the Denishawn School of Dancing and Related Arts, which is considered the first modern dance school in the world.

that are socially, culturally, and individually constructed, which in turn contribute an inadequate aesthetic experience in physical education programs. The process of feminization through dance (Brennan, 1993) and masculinization through sports (Connell, 1989) is deeply rooted in our society. While some researchers point out that activities of emotional sharing are not favoured by boys, Flintoff (1991) goes further by suggesting that boys often purposely distance themselves from any feminine activities (such as dance) and opt instead for activities which can define their masculinity (such as sports). Although not all people oppose boys' participation in dance, the implication of dance as a feminine activity or one preferred by homosexuals indeed influences boys in their viewing of, thinking about, and participating in dance or related activities (Flintoff, 1991). That might partially explain why there are so few males in dance.

Lori-Ann Palen (2008) and Wayne Martino (1999) have each published numerous studies showing that adolescents easily reject those who disagree with them and form their own theory to justify and legitimize what they do. In this context, it is understandable that the only boy in his first dance class might want to quit after dancing with 35 girls. He simply could not mention his dancing and portray himself (a male dance student) as a "normal" boy to his classmates, who are not involved in dance. It is difficult for him to legitimize and justify his own actions (participating in a dance class) under such circumstances. Consequently, his decision to quit dance might seem inevitable. Another observation showed further evidence. In September 2014, the University of Macau held a dance recruitment event on its brand-new campus in Hengqin, China. Nearly 50 students attended the audition and among them were two boys. One left at the beginning of the audition, claiming that he had entered the "wrong room." The other boy quit in the middle of the audition without saying anything. It was not a lack of ability that caused them to leave, as the boy who stayed for half of the audition showed significant potential in dance. The fact that he was the only boy in the room made him feel uncomfortable and so quitting seemed to be a logical solution. It was the same feeling I had experienced 30 years earlier when I first stepped into the dance studio.

Interestingly, a similar gender dilemma exists in high school choirs. Adler (2002) studied adolescent males in choirs at high schools. He discovered an attitude "switch" among adolescent males participating in choir. In his study, he found that young males love to sing only until they reach early adolescence. Once they are in high school and have the opportunity to choose courses, they are not likely to choose choir as their first elective option. This trend can also be seen in extracurricular activities such as Christmas choir at school or school-based dance companies. Adler further asserts that boys in a school choir are likely to be bullied. Many of these young males are afraid of being labelled as gays or girlish boys. Voice and dance teachers in both high schools and universities face the same situation: there are very few young males in their courses. It is challenging because the lower the number of male participants in these fields, the less likely other males are to choose to enter these classes.

Gard and Meyenn (2000) did a research study with a group of junior high school boys (age 11–14) on their preferences for different physical activities as a way to identify themselves. Not surprisingly, dance was rated the lowest or close to the lowest among all. What was interesting was that when two or three boys were interviewed together, their responses/ comments toward dance turned increasingly negative as if they were trying to define their masculinity as men or declare sexuality as being not a gay. Gard and Meyenn's research implied that boys are simply attempting to establish their identity within a "heavily gendered social hierarchy in which dance is associated with homosexuality and where homosexuality is considered abnormal and inferior to heterosexuality" (p. 217). Ted Shawn, one of the pioneers in modern dance in the early twentieth century, spent almost his whole lifetime making male dancers more accepted in the United States. Despite his efforts, male dancers to this day have continued to be considered "effeminate, trivial, and deviant" (Gard, 2003a, p. 211). Thus, it is not difficult to see that adolescent male students struggle with their self-identity and their public identity (the way male dance students see themselves through the public lens). It is the interplay between these two identities that can have an impact on students' involvement and attitude in dance training at high schools.

Despite the positive and encouraging research studies showing clear advantages for males in dance when it comes to job opportunities and promotion (Benoit, 2000; Berger, 2003; Burt, 1995, 1998; Milner, 2002), most males deliberately choose not to dance. There indeed can be many excuses for quitting or avoiding involvement in dance, as numerous studies have suggested. Questions about why males don't dance specific forms or choose to move in particular ways or to different kinds of music would generate some interesting answers. However, I doubt that it will lead to meaningful solutions to remediate the current gender imbalance in dance. It is problematic when males avoiding or quitting dance is perceived as normal.

Some scholars suggest that the low number of male dance teachers as role models has directly caused the sparse enrolment of male dance participants (Gard, 2001; Gilbert, 2003). That argument depends on which institutions you consider in terms of gender representation in teaching faculties. In general, there are more females teaching dance, but males excel in other dance areas. Burt (2007) suggests that although fewer males are in dance, they usually represent the power in the profession. In his book *The Male Dancer: Bodies, Spectacle, Sexualities*, Burt states that in Western countries, fewer men are trained to be professional dancers than women, but many of those men have carried greater responsibilities in dance. These few male dancers eventually occupy most of the important positions as choreographers and artistic directors in their field. Burt's claim of such super male power is clearly shown in the Toronto dance community – with Michael Trent,[2] James Kudelka,[3] Christopher House,[4] and Danny Grossman,[5] just to name a few. It is important to acknowledge that many of these dance companies are founded by female dancers but eventually controlled by males (Warner, 2010).

Dance Education in Schools

Schools (especially public schools) are important places for the regulation and normalization of student bodies and subjectivities, which inevitably promote, demote, or legitimize certain ways of doing or thinking (Connell, 1993; Kirk, 1993, 1998). Overall in public schools, dance is not seen as an important part of school life (Gard, 2008).

The Toronto District School Board, the largest school board in Canada, has only a few schools that consistently provide students with regular dance courses (TDSB, 2009a).[6] Nonetheless, TDSB is considered to be one of the "Arts Enriched" school boards that is envied by many smaller school boards in the province. Carmelina Martin, president of

---

2 Artistic director of Dancemaker Dance Company (Trent, 2008).
3 Former artistic director of the National Ballet of Canada (The National Ballet of Canada, 2015).
4 Artistic director of the Toronto Dance Theatre (House, 2008).
5 Artistic director of the Danny Grossman Dance Company (Grossman, 2007).
6 Downsview Secondary School, Etobicoke School of the Arts, Earl Haig Secondary School, Rosedale Heights School of the Arts, Danforth Collegiate and Technical Institute (C & TI), Woburn Collegiate Institute (CI), and Wexford School for the Arts.

the Pulse Ontario Youth Dance Conference,[7] says that some school boards in Ontario do not have any arts-focused schools. It is justifiable and understandable that different subject areas have their own communities of practice within schools. Some critical educators and researchers who are actively involved in multiple disciplines indicate that the whole process of regulation, normalization, promotion, or legitimization of certain courses produces and reproduces unjust educational and social experiences and leads to inequitable outcomes (Acker, 1994; Hooks, 1994; McLaren, 1999; Willis, 1981). The neglect of dance education in public schools most likely plays a part in the lack of interest towards dance among adolescent males. Nevertheless, research studies clearly show the benefit of including dance in education.

Dance Curriculum

Dance is an important component of a school curriculum because it gives students an opportunity to gain control of their body and mind through "creative accomplishment." In dance, students learn "principles of controlling and organizing movement in space and time" (d'Amboise & Seham, 1994, p. 2). They also explore the concepts of shape and energy through different movements, gestures, and steps. These habits and skills enable students to excel not only in dance but also in many other areas. The Ontario dance curriculum acknowledges that dance and other arts subjects "play a valuable role in the education of all students. Through participation in the arts, students can develop their creativity, learn about their own identity, and develop self-awareness, self-confidence, and a sense of well-being" (*The Arts: The Ontario Curriculum, Grades 9 and 10*, 2010, p. 3). The curriculum promotes inclusiveness and welcomes all who are interested in learning dance, especially those with little or no dance background. It "introduces students to the notions that movement is a medium of expression and that the human body is an instrument. Dance transforms images, ideas, and feelings into movement sequences" (p. 49). The curriculum allows educators to teach Western dance forms such as modern, ballet, jazz, and tap while promoting multicultural dance (African, Chinese, etc.), creative dance, and popular

---

7 Pulse Ontario Youth Dance Conference is the largest school-based dance conference in Ontario, Canada. Its biannual conference is held at York University's state-of-the-art dance facility and attracts hundreds of participants. For more information, visit www.pulsedance.ca.

dance forms (including krump, lock, twist, and more). The curriculum document strives to demystify dance education, and it emphasizes that artistic activities are closely connected to play and human interaction.

> Students experience a sense of wonder and joy when engaged in the arts, which can motivate them to participate more fully in cultural life and in other educational opportunities. Dance education goes beyond studying a repertoire of movements to offering an understanding of the principles and concepts that govern and define the arts. (*The Arts: The Ontario Curriculum, Grades 11 and 12*, 2010)

Dance is a subject area in the Ontario school curriculum. At the high school level, students can take dance as an elective course towards their high school diploma. In elementary schools, dance is usually combined with drama and taught by classroom teachers for a variety of reasons. The majority of primary school teachers in the province of Ontario (junior kindergarten to grade 8) have to teach all subjects, which include math, history, language, all arts disciplines (visual arts, music, drama, and dance), and more. Dance in this case is often taught by availability, such as by a qualified dance educator in the school (as with artists-in-residence programs) or a certified classroom teacher who has a dance background. Artists-in-residence programs in Ontario are not funded by the government, so schools have to find their own resources to fill this position. That creates inequality, as affluent neighbourhoods can usually raise more money to sustain such programs than underprivileged or immigrant neighbourhoods, where less money may be generated. According to a recent survey, general classroom teachers in Ontario, especially at the elementary level, are not teaching dance curriculum because of a lack of experience, skills, and comfort level. Many classroom teachers have concerns that teaching dance would take away their time from regular programs, which place a lot of emphasis on literacy and numeracy. In summary, despite the existence of the dance curriculum, many Ontario schools do not offer dance classes.

Dance was merely a component within the physical education curriculum in the 1970s. It was often taught not by physical education teachers but by dance artists outside of school through workshops (what would now be seen as artists-in-residence programs). Later on, dance became a unit in the curriculum, along with physical activity, healthy living, and others. In the 1980s, dance was separated from physical education, and it became more visible among high schools and universities. This move created a positive result in a number of ways: more weight in the curriculum, increased participation (teachers and students), artist-teacher involvement, government funding, and an emphasis on developing creativity and critical thinking through the arts. In the mid-1990s, dance and drama were introduced into *The Arts* curriculum as one subject area, which remained controversial for a number of years. Dance was an independent subject in the high school curriculum, but it had to be combined with drama at the elementary level. Prior to the introduction of the dance curriculum, various interests groups including physical education teachers, university and professional dance schools, and curriculum and policy writers debated the merits of combining dance with drama, including it in physical education, or teaching it as its own discipline until dance finally became a separate curriculum subject in elementary schools as well.

Within four decades, dance has evolved from a component in physical education programs to an independent subject area in Ontario's *The Arts* curriculum. Despite the rapid changes in the curriculum, dance is still a marginalized subject area. Few public schools in Ontario, especially at the elementary level, offer dance courses to students. Those schools that have dance studios, performance space, and qualified dance educators (arts-focused high schools) usually require auditions for entrance. Auditions discriminate against students who want to take dance in high school but who have little or no dance background. In other words, underprivileged students are being penalized for not having dance training and therefore are disqualified to learn dance in high school. Ironically, the reality of dance education in Ontario schools fails to acknowledge what health specialists – including the World Health Organization – dance scholars, and curriculum consultants have been advocating for years: the benefits of dancing, which include increased physical activity, mental/physical health, teamwork, self-esteem, and problem solving.

In the midst of all of these issues, Rosedale Heights School of the Arts, which requires no audition and welcomes anyone regardless of their background, stands out. More relevant to this study, the number of male students in dance at Rosedale has increased dramatically over the years because its dance program does not focus solely on technique and competitiveness, but instead emphasizes basic dance skills, teamwork, and social interaction. All these attributes have made this inclusive dance program grow rapidly, especially in terms of attracting and keeping males involved. The school is quite a contrast to the school I attended: no audition, freedom to select courses, either academic or arts subjects, and it does not pressure anyone to become an artist. This unique and open approach is not comparable to Chinese dance schools, which emphasize technique, body figures, and appearance. Yet it attracts students and allows them to take or consider taking dance regardless of their age, body shape, and appearance. Nonetheless, I still wonder, if I were a student at Rosedale, would I have become who I am today? What if I were born in Toronto and went to an arts school that required an audition, such as Etobicoke School of the Arts? Would that make any difference?

Guidelines and Gender Presentation in Dance Education

Throughout the research process, I used the Ontario curriculum document *The Arts* as my guideline and main source of reference. This particular document, revised and published in 2009, is the standard document for all teachers in Ontario, and it lists all expectations that students at different grade levels should meet. In November 2006, the Ontario government began to review its arts curriculum in anticipation of releasing the new curriculum in 2009. For the dance/drama division, 24 dance specialists were selected across the province; I was one of the representatives from the city of Toronto. It was an opportunity to meet and consult with dance representatives from all regions of Ontario.

During the curriculum revision process, some expressed concerns about the complexity of the language in the current curriculum. I was more concerned with but not surprised to see the extreme imbalanced gender presentation on the curriculum revision committee: 23 females and 1 male, me. I had often been the lone male participant at such events as dance conferences, seminars, and workshops on equity in dance. During this particular curriculum review, numerous recommendations were put forward with no mention of gender imbalance or ways of promoting males' participation in dance. From my point of view, this curriculum revision did not make any progress in terms of promoting dance among all, especially males. It simplified some terminologies, provided teaching examples, and linked to online resources. It did not fundamentally solve the core problem – promoting gender equity in dance education. Nonetheless, the newly revised curriculum highlighted the benefits and the positive impact of dance in the curriculum, which has been championed by researchers around the globe. In Stinson's (1991) study, she investigates why students dance and discovers that many students choose to take dance because in dance classes they gain "the sense of power and control over themselves, the transcendence or high" (p. 24). Dance as a curriculum subject promotes feelings of competence and inspires excitement, interest in school, and higher achievement goals (Hanna, 1989; Weissberg, Caplan, & Harwood, 1991). Dance students are especially "supportive, applauding, cheering," and they shout out encouragement when others are dancing or performing (Seham, 1997, p. 9). This is crucial because students' "self-esteem and the concept of self depend on reflected appraisal" from others (Minuchin, Montalvo, Guerney, Rusman, & Schumer, 1967, p. 221). Studies of New York public schools with a dance program show an increased sense of specialness, capability, confidence, and empowerment among elementary school students. Schmitz (1990) states, "The engagement in dance activities provides a meaningful way for students to develop motor control, basic body concepts, verbal and kinaesthetic understandings, spatial relationships, and inter- and intro-personal relationships" (p. 61). Schmitz's study also confirms that students' attitude towards school, attendance, sense of responsibility, behaviour, work ethic, and academic achievement improved while participating in dance. Dance as part of the curriculum in schools creates positive outcomes for students. These positive effects of dance are not novel findings and have been featured in movies, including *Mad Hot Ballroom* (Agrelo & Sewell, 2005) and *Take the Lead* (Friedlander, 2006). Margolin's (2008) research study was completed in the school context under the guidelines of the Ontario curriculum document. She led a series of creative movement workshops for female inner-city high school students in Toronto and found that creative dance plays an important role in helping these girls access important bodily knowledge, which led to deepened self-understanding, self-worth, and relationships with their peers and family members. Nonetheless, some of the benefits and skills developed in dance are similar to those developed in physical education. Could a physical education program be enough?

Dance and Physical Education

In the past few decades, there have been frequent arguments about whether dance should be included in the physical education program (Deluzio, 1998; Flores, 1995; Foregger & Miller, 1975; Sallis et al., 1997). In the province of Ontario, dance is separated from physical education and health, but the separation did not come easily. In 1998, when the former ruling Conservative government tried to push through educational reform policies (Bill 160), dance was intended to be part of the physical education program. However, under fierce public pressure and non-stop phone calls from parents, artists, teachers, school trustees, and administrators, the government reversed its decision to include dance as part of the physical education curriculum just days before the policy was launched (Deluzio, 2009). The majority of adolescent males I interviewed confessed that they participated in physical education in the past only because they did not have a choice. Many of them saw dance as an activity for female students and sports as an activity for males. I began to wonder whether more boys would take dance if dance was subsumed under physical education.

In many Ontario secondary schools where dance is not offered, school and school board administrators have suggested that physical education teachers deliver a dance "component" as part of the physical education course. They have presented previous studies to argue their views on the combination of dance and physical education programs. Stevens (1992) advocates that the inclusion of dance in physical education would provide overall benefits to student participants. Glaister (1987) adds that dance in physical education "teaches a child to dance instead of teaching him/her a dance." Dance inserts an aesthetic and artistic element to physical education, which is considered a new approach to educate "the whole child" (Roundell, 2002).

Based on this theoretical framework, dance seems to be an excellent add-on to the physical education program. Nevertheless, a problem emerges when physical education teachers see dance as just one of the many components they have to teach. There is then the danger of dance becoming just a technique or a kind of skill acquisition, which can be taught the same way that baseball, soccer, or basketball is taught. Teaching dance involves much more than just learning a dance piece so that specific curriculum expectations are fulfilled. Teaching dance is about enabling students to physically explore a different culture and to learn a region or country's value, history, geography, aesthetics, social, and economic issues.

Bleakley and Brennan (2008) assert that in physical education classes that have to include dance, the aesthetic and artistic approach in dance is often not valued or appreciated by the physical education teachers (regardless of gender). Most of them, if not all, choose not to include dance in their physical education program. Lloyd and West (1988) believe that it is due to physical education teachers' own inadequate knowledge of and experience in dance. As a result, negative consequences arise. Gard (2001) claims that boys need rhythmical and physical training and that they will respond to dance as long as it is not decreed as a "sissy" activity or as long as they are not asked to dance effeminate movements. As an educator, I suspect that dance would face extreme challenges to survive in a regular physical education course because it would be constantly ignored no matter how much theorists and administrators argued for it.

Numerous studies have shown that increased physical activity has resulted in decreased cardiovascular disease (Powell, Thompson, Caspersen, & Kendrick, 1987). Increased physical activity also contributes to better weight control and a healthy body (Baranowski, 1992; Kelder, Perry, & Klepp, 1993). Despite the positive outcomes from physical activities, some studies suggest that physical education classes actually offer a limited amount of physical activity. Children in general spend less than 10 per cent of their physical education time in moderate to vigorous activity, on average amounting to less than 10 minutes per week (Simons-Morton, Taylor, Snider, & Huang, 1993). In my previous study, many students stated that they were less likely to feel fatigue while moving with music and travelling within a space with challenging and stimulating sequences, compared to common physical education activities (Li, 2007).

One significant difference between physical education and dance education is the gender of the educators. While both genders are likely to be represented among those who teach physical education, one is much less likely to see males teaching dance, especially in public schools. Studies show that in general females are more likely to choose teaching as a profession than males are (Blount, 2000; O'Donnell, 1984). The gender imbalance is exceptionally worse in dance education, and there is a great need for skilled male dance teachers to attract and keep young male students engaged (Benoit, 2000; Berger, 2003; Grady, 2002). Talbot (1993) states that in order to address equity issues in dance education, we must consider factors such as gender in the teaching profession and teaching methods. Female dance teachers overshadow their male counterparts in large numbers for a variety of reasons. Scholars including Foulkes (2001), Keyworth (2001), Marques (1998), and Mirault (2000) have suggested that it is crucial to have male dance educators teaching dance. Male dance instructors who could lead high-energy and well-rounded dance classes would contribute to a quality experience that in return would successfully expand adolescent boys' narrow perceptions of masculinity (Brennan, 1996). Having male dance teachers could also break down stereotypes that males should not dance.

While the lack of male dance instructors seems to be a problem, the method in which dance is actually "presented and delivered" is much more crucial in its acceptance among adolescent boys (Brennan, 1996, p. 495). Lipscomb (1986) notes that a regular dance class warm-up, which usually emphasizes flexibility and coordination, is often the reason boys have rejected participating in dance. Brennan (1996) states that "female PE [physical education] has centered on educating the child through the physical while male PE is more concerned with performance and success ... Women specialists who take on the task of teaching dance to mixed classes now have to re-evaluate their teaching materials, resources, and models in order to compensate for differences in experience and level of competence" (p. 496). She further suggests that all dance instructors, male and female, should reassess their teaching methodologies and pay extra attention to what adolescent male dance students really need or enjoy. Similar arguments and pedagogical approaches to dance education are shared by other scholars (Bond, 1994; Gard, 2001; Marques, 1998). For instance, a front split[8] during the stretching section or the twisting upper body movements in a jazz warm-up should probably be modified to accommodate male students. Instead, an intense session of sit-ups and push-ups would fulfil the same warm-up purpose, and peer stretching would work better than asking boys to do a split.

Moving Boys into Dance

Can the employment of male dance educators or modification of teaching strategies really change the tide so that more males will participate in or continue to take dance? On the one hand, we want to encourage more boys to participate, but on the other, if teaching methods were restructured just for boys' needs, new problems might surface. First, in order to attract boys, we may purposely exaggerate or add "extra strength" to certain moves or gestures to avoid a commonly perceived "feminized" look. Male dance students may then start to perceive this way of training as the "manly" way and other male students who are not trained this way as "feminine" or "homosexual." Martino (1999) challenges such "simplistic conceptualization of boys as a homogeneous group whose interests are set against those of girls" (p. x). In fact, this study has found that some boys choose to take dance because they just enjoy doing it, regardless of styles and its appearance. Second, to say that male teachers

---

8 A front split is usually performed when a dancer holds one leg in front of the body and the other leg is behind.

attract more male students may give the wrong impression that female dance teachers are not able to teach male dance students. That is simply not true. Scholars (Benoit, 2000; Berger, 2003; Crawford, 1994; Grady, 2002) suggest that having a male dance teacher helps keep males in dance, yet there are indeed many well-established professional male dancers who have been taught by both female and male dance teachers. Regardless of the gender of the teacher, these males stayed and succeeded in the profession. Third, we may indirectly promote certain dance styles, hence creating imbalanced dance training and generating a "phobia" attitude towards other dance forms. For instance, teaching hip hop and breakdance is an excellent way to attract males and keep males in dance. At the same time, are we saying that males cannot do ballet or lyrical jazz or that girls should not do hip hop and breakdance? Attracting males and keeping them in dance involves careful consideration of outcomes; it is more than just the gender of the teacher and changing the types of movements taught. To effectively attract and keep adolescent males in dance, dance educators should start to pay attention to how they think about dance rather than why they should dance. When we change the why to how, it might result in better outcomes for males in dance.

Gard (2008) has looked very closely at the how and why questions through a multitude of pedagogical approaches to dance education. He suggests that "dance educators should seriously consider HOW students, especially males, experience, think, and feel about dance rather than WHY they should dance" (p. 181). Researchers have presented numerous studies on the benefits and positive outcomes that dance could bring to human beings (Benoit, 2000; Roenigk, 2003). That list includes self-confidence, good coordination, proper posture, rhythm, and more. Bond and Stinson (2000–1) have collected data from approximately 600 students (age 3–18) from Australia, Canada, Spain, and the United States with an emphasis on young people's feelings while dancing. They state that "many young people reported feelings of heightened self, rising above limitations and boundaries" (p. 76). Bond and Stinson's study is a good starting point to understand the how questions in dance. It is this exploration that may really be the missing piece to the puzzle of the gender imbalance in dance. With dance now as a separate subject in the curriculum, it is a step in the right direction and perhaps may even set the stage for the entrance of more young male dancers.

3
Where Are the Dancing Boys?

I taught dance from 2003 to 2014 at Rosedale Heights School of the Arts, where its dance program had a healthy number of male participants. Does gender of the dance teacher affect students' willingness to take dance? We will discuss this question in later chapters. As the only full-time male dance teacher in the Toronto District School Board, I had a challenging time locating male dance students in other schools. In particular, I was looking at those adolescent males who took dance in non-professional schools. In Toronto, I contacted Downsview Secondary School, Etobicoke School of the Arts, Earl Haig Secondary School, Danforth C & TI, Woburn CI, and Wexford School for the Arts, where dance is offered. I also spoke to high school dance teachers in other Canadian cities such as Waterloo (Eastwood Collegiate Institute), Halifax (Citadel High School), and Vancouver (Gladstone Secondary School). A pre-professional dance training centre (the School of Toronto Dance Theatre) and post-secondary institutions (York University and George Brown College) were also on my enquiry list. Hoping to collect a large database, I reached out to a few secondary schools in the United States that offered dance classes. However, findings were not encouraging. The lack of adolescent male dance students was common, both in big cities like Toronto and New York and in small towns across Canada and the United States, at secondary schools and at professional dance schools such as Canada's National Ballet School, the School of Toronto Dance Theatre, and Houston Metropolitan Dance Center. Female dance students dominated the classes, usually far surpassing their male counterparts in numbers.

With the help of teaching colleagues, dance artists, and the Internet, I located a public secondary school in Texas in the United States that had an all-boys dance class. I immediately tried to connect with the teacher, principal, and its superintendent, only to find out that the program had been closed for unexplained reasons. This left Rosedale Heights as the only example I could find of a public school that had a separate dance class for male students. Not only did the school have an all-boys dance class, but its male dance student population was also growing so rapidly that it received much attention from the TDSB's arts committee and the Ontario Ministry of Education. There were other arts schools in Toronto and other cities mentioned, but the ratios of males to females were extreme. What happened with Rosedale Heights's male students? Why did they take dance, what was the teaching environment, and did the administration notice this "spike" of males participating in dance? I thought these students might provide great insight about males in dance, such as ways to resist the pressures of gender stereotyping. From them, I wanted to find out what it was like to be an adolescent male dance student at Rosedale Heights. I was fully aware of the fact that these boys took dance in an arts high school (no audition required) and that many were taught by a male dance teacher. In fact, the question of if and how these factors played any role in males' decision to take dance or continue dance training generated some interesting findings, which are discussed in later chapters.

Interviewing the entire male dance student population (about 60) in the school was not realistic or practical. Although there were many males taking dance at Rosedale, they represented only a small portion of all males in dance (Illus. 3.1). In addition to interviewing some of them, I also wanted to look at the location of the school, teaching environment, peer pressure, family structure, administration, and teaching staff. What role did these factors play? Did they exert any influence on adolescent males' decision to take dance in high school? In the end, I chose to carry out a small-group study and used a lottery-based process to select participants to ensure equity and validity. Participants did not know who was or was not involved because all interviews took place during lunchtime and in after-school settings outside the dance studios. The participants were selected from both all-boys and mixed-gender dance classes. Each participant was assigned a pseudonym to protect his privacy and confidentiality.

Rosedale Heights School of the Arts (RHSA) is located in downtown Toronto, Ontario. In 2014 it had a student population of 1,050, a principal, 2 vice principals, and 63 teachers. The school focuses on the arts (dance, drama, music, and visual arts) but it does not require an audition for entry, unlike the majority of performing arts schools in and outside of Toronto. To get into Rosedale, students are asked to write a

Illus. 3.1. Students from the all-boys class dance in front
of Rosedale Heights School of the Arts

statement about why they should be admitted and the reasons they want
to study at this particular school. The school's philosophy is to teach and
transform students with little or no background in the arts into emerg-
ing artists or arts enthusiasts by the time they graduate from high school.
The administration requires all students to take at least two arts courses
each year, chosen from dance, drama, visual arts, and music, in addition
to other academic courses.

Rosedale's dance program teaches three dance styles: jazz, ballet, and
modern. About one third of the school population, or 350–400 students,
take dance; a similar proportion take drama, visual arts, and music.
There are three full-time dance teachers responsible for 16 dance ses-
sions from grade 9 to grade 12. Each class has 25–33 students. No audition is required for students to take dance courses, but teachers do place
students differently according to their skills and levels. This is done mainly
for safety reasons. In dance, the majority of students are beginner dancers, with little or no dance training background prior to high school.
Students choose to attend Rosedale mainly because of their interests or

friends' and parents' recommendations. The dance program focuses on both theory and practice. That means students learn basic technique and skills while studying different theories in dance history, anatomy, choreography, criticism, and maintaining a healthy body. There are regular assignments, quizzes, presentations, performances, and even a final exam for all dance classes. Rosedale's dance program strives to balance students' bodies and minds while showing others (students and teachers) that dance is an area of study, not just a form of entertainment.

Getting males to take dance has always been challenging. In 2003, Rosedale Heights started to offer an all-boys dance class. Since then, the number of male participants in dance has steadily grown. In the 2008–9 school year, there were 55 male dance students; in 2009–10, that number went up to 62. From this group, 12 adolescent male dance students from 16 dance classes were randomly selected to be included in a small study group for this research. Among the participants, 11 were born in Canada; one was born in Costa Rica but came to Canada when he was an infant. Most of the boys were born in Toronto; one was born in British Columbia and two in Edmonton. Please refer to Table 3.1 for a summary of the background information about the participants.[1]

Ethnicity

In this study I wanted to see if ethnicity had any impact on adolescent males' decision to take dance in high school. Since I grew up in China, I used my knowledge of the dance system there to make some comparisons. There seemed to be no apparent discrimination against males who take dance in China, and the number of males seemed to be abundant. Yet, looking closer, I found that the large number of males occurs either at the professional level or in pre-professional dance training institutions. Males in recreational dance programs such as after-school dance clubs and dance studios are scarce. In dance programs in public schools, females significantly outnumber males. This is quite similar to what I have found in many schools in Canada. I suspect that many families (Chinese and Canadian) see dance as a female profession or a hobby, and subsequently the majority of participants in dance are girls. Many mainland Chinese parents wanted their children to be in "professional fields," which were respected, secure, and relatively well-paid. This particular

---

1 Names of all participants have been changed to protect their identity.

Table 3.1. Description of the adolescent male dance students studied

Code	Name	Age	Grade	Ethnicity	Dance experience prior to high school	Dance experience in high school	Takes extra dance training outside the high school	Dance class
1	George	14	10	Caucasian	No	2 years	No	All-boys dance
2	Jim	14	10	African Canadian	1 month	2 years	No	All-boys dance
3	Bruce	14	10	multiracial	No	2 years	No	All-boys dance
4	Michael	16	11	Caucasian	No	3 years	No	All-boys dance
5	David	13	9	Caucasian	No	1 year	No	All-boys dance
6	Tom	14	10	Caucasian	No	2 years	No	All-boys dance
7	Carter	16	11	multiracial	No	2 years	Yes	Mixed-gender dance cla
8	Kyle	13	9	Chinese	No	1 year	No	All-boys dance
9	Wilson	13	9	Caucasian	No	1 year	No	All-boys dance
10	Robert	18	12	Caucasian	1 year	5 years	Yes	Mixed-gender dance cla
11	Liam	14	10	Caucasian	6 months	2 years	Yes	Mixed-gender dance cla
12	Alan	14	10	multiracial	No	2 years	No	All-boys dance

group of parents had a huge influence on their children's school choice, including course selection. When comparing Chinese and Canadian parents, I found that Chinese parents were more goal-oriented and practical. They would support their children's decision only when their choices matched what the parents wanted. Parents might support their children's decision to learn dance for physical benefits, but most would not allow them to pursue it as a career. Not all Chinese parents would do the same, though. One Chinese Canadian parent in this study indicated that she supported her son's involvement in dance and would continue her support if he decided to study dance further. Unfortunately, her son's passion in dance did not last long; he later switched his interest to drama. There was an interesting trend that the longer Chinese Canadian parents stayed in Canada, the more support and freedom they would give their children in terms of dancing. This finding was strengthened by interviewing other male dance students who shared different ethnic backgrounds. Ethnicity did have an impact on young males' decision to take or stay in dance, but it was adjusted as their living environment and culture changed.

In my case, I was one of two boys in a 40-pupil dance class at the beginning. My experience coincided with the research data in Toronto. A few adolescent males in this study stated that they were among few boys when they first took dance before high school. The situation does not improve much when boys grow older, perhaps getting worse as more males choose not to take dance. Teenage girls dominating dance classes is extremely common among amateur dance studios in both China and Canada. The trend is reduced at pre-professional (late adolescence) and professional (after 18) training facilities (dance institutions, company, and gifted schools), where gender discrepancy is less obvious. That is mainly due to each individual institution's requirements, which attempt to accept equal numbers of males and females for entry. This was a common practice in China when I was one of the final choices at a professional dance school. Regardless of students' ethnic background, I found uneven gender representations existed even at pre-professional training facilities in Toronto. For instance, the School of Toronto Dance Theatre, Ballet Creole School, and Etobicoke School of the Arts, among others, had many fewer male students than females. In these institutions, males had different ethnic backgrounds, which made me think that it was perhaps the culture that made dance inaccessible to males. The lack of male dancers at the pre-professional training stage in Canada leads to insufficient supplies of male dancers for dance companies in Canada. National

Ballet of Canada, Toronto Dance Theatre, and Alberta Ballet have all had to hire male dancers from outside Canada. Many of these male dancers were trained in Eastern European and Asian countries. More males are recruited at the pre-professional training stage from these places than countries in the West. In short, I believe that ethnicity does play a role in attracting males to dance. This idea becomes more convincing when certain ethnic groups in Canada (e.g., aboriginals) receive support from government and institutions, including grants, scholarships, and other kinds of assistance, which in turn encourages some males to participate in dance studies.

Ethnic dances are viewed differently among males. For instance, many young male Chinese dance students began with folk dances in after-school clubs and in dance studios. Tibetan or Mongolian dances were particularly appealing to them because of their "tough look" and athletic tricks. People in those regions live, dress, speak, sing, and move differently because of their geographical and cultural environments. At the same time, young boys could appreciate watching a classical ballet such as *The Nutcracker* because it also contained some energetic movement sequences based on folk dance, where the males showed off their high jumps and tricks.

On the other hand, modern dance is considered a Western dance form, not an ethnic dance. It's relatively young, about 100 years old, and still evolving. Many people, both males and females, are still trying to comprehend the concept of this dance form. What did the early modern dancers and choreographers do and why? The lack of males in dance, especially modern male dancers, can be traced back to the early twentieth century. Perhaps that is why Ted Shawn established his all-male dance company in the United States, which unfortunately did not last long. His attempt to re-establish males' glory in dance failed, partially due to the war and ingrained socially constructed thought that men should not dance. Nonetheless, Ramsay Burt (1995) found that immediately after the First World War, "there were a number of men working as dancers and choreographers in modern dance styles in Germany" (p. 6). Limited documentation and language barriers have left that piece of history almost untraceable. I cannot explain why so many men danced in Germany. Burt later pointed out that male bodies in Western countries were seen as a taboo subject for cultural representation from around 1830 until around 1980. I would argue that his view on males in dance still resonates with many young males today. Canadian dance companies

Fig. 3.1. Ethnicity of adolescent male dance students

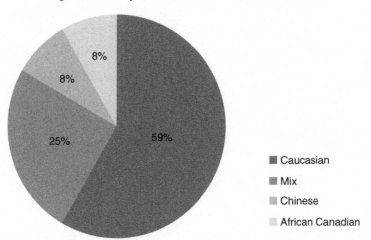

have benefited from the influx of talented immigrants since the 1950s. Many foreign-trained male dancers have been hired by local dance companies. I believe this has led to even fewer local males wanting to pursue dance because they are pessimistic about their career opportunities. Some of the adolescent male dance students in this study admitted that they were too "old" to be trained as highly technical dancers, compared to those who started dance at a much younger age. One male student who studied dance at the National Ballet School later gave up dance entirely because he felt that he had "no chance" of being hired as a dancer. This highlights the need to pay more attention and to provide more support to pre-professional training facilities, including high school and even elementary school, to encourage more young males to participate in dance. That means all males, regardless of their age and ethnic background. In this research, 7 out of 12 students were Caucasian, three multiracial, one Chinese, and one African Canadian. Among all of the boys who took dance at Rosedale, the majority were Caucasians, while others' ethnic roots extended to countries all over the world. The demographic of the chosen group almost perfectly mirrored the ethnic representations of the male dance community at Rosedale Heights School of the Arts (Fig. 3.1).

Fig. 3.2. Professions of parents of adolescent male dance students

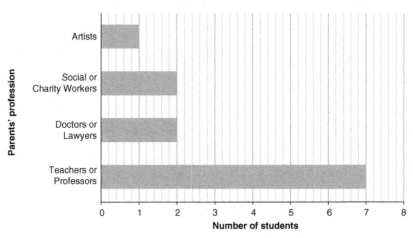

Family

All of the study participants were living with their parents at the time of the research. Most of them had two parents and some siblings at home. More than half of them came from well-educated or so-called middle- or upper-class families. As shown in Fig. 3.2, seven had at least one parent who was a teacher or college professor. Two students' parents were doctors or lawyers. Two indicated that their parents were in some form of social work with an international humanitarian organization. Among all the male dance students in the study, only one participant identified his family as "artsy" (his father was a creative director in a film production company).

On social, financial, and educational grounds, it seemed that this was an elite group of children whose parents supported them in extracurricular activities, including dance classes. Yet the majority of participants expressed that they had never danced before and that it was their first time dancing in high school. These findings show that educated parents from relatively affluent families were more open to dance. Dance offered as a credit course towards a high school diploma also provided adolescent males with a legitimate excuse to experience dance. Parents, in return, were more likely to support such decisions.

Stories

Stories revealed from interviewing these adolescent male dance students allowed me to gain insight into their views on dance, gender, choreography, and performance and how these elements function in society. The tales embedded in the students' minds, bodies, and movements are essential and authentic ways to inform those who are bewildered by the phenomenon of gender imbalance in dance. Through these interviews, it gradually became clear why these adolescent males took dance and what made them enjoy dancing.

The one-on-one interviews were conducted on three separate occasions using a semi-structured interview guide. The first interviews took place before classroom observations began. This is the time when new students (grade 9) begin and older students resume dance training. More interview questions were asked when the first semester was drawing to an end. The last interviews were conducted in June after the students had just completed their year-end dance performance. Each interview lasted approximately 30 minutes, and all took place on school premises during after-school hours or at the convenience of those being interviewed.

Interviews with parents were used to find out whether there was a correlation between their son's preference and the final decision to take dance at high school. I chose to interview the parents as well because family is the most crucial element of socialization in all societies. Also, by using a semi-structured interview guide, the interviews looked into whether the parents' thoughts on their son's involvement in dance had ever changed. Furthermore, through these interviews I attempted to find out and to document their son's comments and feelings on their dance experience at high school. The majority of interviews took place during regularly scheduled parent-teacher interviews. Some additional interviews were arranged after school or at parents' convenience. Each interview lasted approximately 20 minutes. Parents were informed that they did not have to respond to any questions which they might feel uncomfortable answering.

Artefacts

Student assignments were seen as artefacts to understand how students applied their physical embodiment (dance) to their analytical, reflective, and critical thinking in theoretical ways (mind). When they were asked about their favourite activities in dance during the year, answers varied. Most of the junior students (just beginning dancing) opted for the culminating activity, which was performing on the stage, whereas seniors (who had danced for at least one year) chose the Dancer & Me assignment. Assignments were created with the guidelines of the Ontario curriculum, *The Arts*, with a specific focus on male dancers. All assignments were distributed throughout the school year, but only selected ones were documented and analysed. Examining assignments was a way to understand adolescent males' analytical and reflective understanding about dance in general. Some assignments (e.g., Dancer & Me and journals) were more relevant to this research project than others (e.g., dance history and movement vocabularies).

The Blog

In this research, the use of digital data (the Internet) was an important way of collecting the students' responses. The blog assignment was an in-class activity which required students to post anonymous responses to dance clips online. Every student in the all-boys dance classes participated in this student-to-student online activity in a school computer lab. To start, I posted questions or topics for discussion. For instance, during one of the blogging sections, I posted the question, Why did you choose to take dance in high school? I noticed that because they did not know each other's identity, students were more enthusiastic to reveal their stories in dance. Many students shared intriguing stories, but only those belonging to the small focus group of 12 were used in this research. On another occasion, I posted a YouTube clip of a Toronto Dance Theatre performance and an episode of *So You Think You Can Dance*, students were then invited to critique their dance pieces and choreographic structure (e.g., things they liked and disliked). Students were allowed to complete this assignment either during the class or after school at their own convenience. I designed it this way because some students needed more time to write out their thoughts on dance while others simply preferred to work at home. Students who chose to submit their response at their own convenience would jot down notes while watching the clips during the class.

I included the blogging for three reasons. One was to get an overall response regarding their involvement in dance; it allowed me to do a crosscheck of the data I gathered from the small-group interviews. Another reason was to engage them in dance reviewing activities. Over the years, I noticed that it was challenging to convince boys to purchase tickets to see a live dance performance and then to write a dance review. I adopted this technology of letting students watch dance clips online to promote an interest in watching dance and writing about dance. I found that students did better when the activities were hands-on and technology-based. When we were online, students showed more interest and they were more committed to completing their work.

The major difference with blogging was that it allowed student-to-student interactions. With the help of blogging online, male dance students unveiled some matters that they otherwise would not have discussed in public, such as their dance experiences in childhood that affected their decision to take dance in high school; what they wanted to achieve in dance; how they felt when they danced; what made them continue/discontinue dance; what they wanted to tell others about males in dance; how they understood and used movements to convey a meaningful message; their view on an all-boys dance class compared to a mixed-gender dance class; and what dance meant to them as young male dancers. Blogging strengthened the authenticity of my findings by allowing male dance students to speak openly and frankly. Compared with traditional means, using digital data and posting instant messages on the blog was effective. The responses from the students were positive and the students were fully engaged with the topic, something they admitted that they were not comfortable speaking about in public. Marilyn Olander (2007) is an expert in computing technology in education. In her writing, "Painting the Voice: Weblogs and Writing Instruction in the High School Classroom," she claims that in the classroom, computers and computer-related technology are leading the way both for students and for new approaches to learning, with schools lagging behind. Adolescents are familiar with today's technological trends such as the use of blogging on the Internet. Thomas Carroll (2000) elaborates that the goal for change (technology advancement) should be not to build communities of individual students but to connect communities in which students learn from their peers in collaborative and cooperative relationships rather than in the "traditional transmissive, teacher-centered, fixed curriculum mode" (p. 140). John Dewey (2007) stated that students are motivated to act for purposes of inherent value to them. The blog is one of the more current forms of multimedia for social interactions and has the potential to serve a complete range of technical and instructional goals. Given the comfort of many teenagers with technology, students were indeed more motivated to express themselves through technology than through traditional ways.

Arts-informed Research

As previously mentioned, this book seeks to answer the question, what is it like to be an adolescent male dance student in school today? Much of the methodological focus is on interviews and observation of classroom activities, which include dance. I consider this approach "arts-based" in two specific ways: (1) it intentionally uses artistic activity to evoke data; and (2) it represents the knowledge generated within the study in artistic ways.

Elliot Eisner (2002) writes in his book *The Arts and the Creation of Mind*, "methodological pluralism rather than methodological monism is the ideal to which artistic approaches to research subscribe … looking through one eye never did provide much depth of field" (p. 9). The artistic dimension of data evocation and knowledge representation functions as the other eye to my approach in understanding young males in dance. Themes, actions, movements, and rehearsals that emerge in dance classes make up the information for my enquiry process, which is informed by investigating creative activities such as dancing, improvising, and choreographing. This form of investigation in turn allows me to gain a deeper understanding of the message as communicated by movements, which would otherwise not be as readily available through traditional text-based forms. In this milieu, an arts-based approach is realistic and tangible, and it works both as a process and as a representational form rather than creating an artwork for the sake of art.

During the research, students had to complete a multimedia/visual component for their Dancer & Me assignment. One student created and performed a rap song, and other students either drew a picture or carved a sculpture. Students used their artistic creation as a means to express their views on dance. Their artwork further informed my understanding of the realities of adolescent male dancers. I used my understanding from the arts-based data evocation process as one way to choreograph their year-end dance piece, which not only provides a live, visual, simultaneous, emotional, and physical re-creation and representation of the written text, but can also add meaning to the text itself.

Performance

The performance, the year-end dance piece titled *I Am a Male and I Can Dance*, was choreographed specifically to communicate the meaning of this book. It could be seen as a culmination of all the data into a

Illus. 3.2. A senior dance student from a mixed-gender class dances
with an all-boys class at year-end performance

message from the male dance students and from me, the author and a
male dancer myself. During the three-month rehearsal period, I studied
whether the students' perception of dance changed, how it changed, and
how they viewed themselves before beginning, during rehearsal, and after
the performance.

Performance enquiry is a fusion of imagination and embodiment of
an individual's identity, which is represented in and through dancing. I
apply this enquiry to highlight adolescent male dancers' self-realization,
a state of "optimal flow" which I believe can occur during their dance
performance on stage. Peggy Phelan (1993) describes this self-realization
using the metaphor of a bridge that connects the world of the conscious
(known) to the world of imagination (unknown). During the course of a
performance, the dancers explore, define, and redefine their identities
by using their embodied movements between the two worlds.

To these students, performing a dance on stage in front of a large audience was an extraordinary experience, one that most young males do
not have. After months of rehearsing in dance classes and after-school
practices, students have the opportunity to perform their journeys in

dance and through dance on stage: their journey from having no experience in dance to performing, from feeling embarrassed to bravely expressing themselves through movements, from disliking dance to being a dance enthusiast, from looking down on male dancers to becoming advocates for dance to other male students. This particular experience allows young males to express themselves on stage. While performing, they reveal their inner ideas and feelings about dance, self-identity, and issues that concern them the most (Illus. 3.2).

As they are dancing on stage, both the minds and bodies of these young males are actively engaged. The body is an instrument, and the movements are the vocabulary for them to generate meaning and to communicate with spectators. During the creating, rehearsing, and performing process, adolescent male dance students access their knowledge of the body by living in it and engaging in bodily movements. As a dance teacher and an advocate for young male dancers, I consider performance an authentic, visible, and therefore powerful means not only to keep them in dance but also to entice other adolescent male students to participate in dance. Performance in this case stands alone as a compelling instrument for communication with audiences and readers.

4

The Voices of the Dancing Boys

Many academic studies and popular culture recognize dance as a way of promoting feelings of competence and excitement. However, it is rarely seen that adolescent males share their personal experience in dance verbally with their families and friends. Adolescent males become even more reluctant to talk about their dance experience when they encounter people with whom they are not familiar. It might be that they are afraid of being labelled "abnormal" or "gay" (Berger, 2003; Gard, 2008). My research found different reasons for boys not wanting to dance. Many boys in this study were less likely to speak about dance simply because they were not familiar with the subject. They either started dance late (in high school) or felt isolated as a result of the extreme ratio of males to females in dance. Findings showed that if there were more dance activities in schools, particularly at the elementary level, dance would probably not be seen as a "scary" subject for boys later on. Dance became a positive experience for boys at Rosedale Heights because the school provided them with a safe place to participate in dance, either in all-boys dance classes or mixed-gender dance classes. The majority of male dance students in Rosedale took dance to gain a high school credit. Few expressed that they would choose dance as a career option in the future. However, these boys were not afraid of taking dance because they were among other males, dancing together.

Dancer & Me Assignment

The Dancer & Me assignment was distributed to male grade 9 and 10 dance students at the beginning of the school year. They were asked to apply a variety of means to interpret their current state in dance and to describe how they saw dance as male dance students. It included both a visual (e.g., painting, video, pictures, website) and a written component, in which students explained their motives for creating the visual component or explored their journey in dance and subsequent discoveries. The written component permitted me to gain a better understanding of each student's views on dance. My all-boys dance classes have done this assignment for three years. It showcases adolescent males' analytical and reflective understanding of dance as well as being a tool for students to explore and define their identity in dance. I considered this a hands-on and student-driven assignment; at the same time, it helped me find out where the students were in dance and what they thought about dance.

The Dancer & Me assignment showed that given the right platform, adolescent males could apply multidisciplinary methods to express their thoughts on dance. Junior students in the all-boys dance class were quite resentful of the project at the beginning because it required self-reflection. However, they were proud of what they accomplished in the end. They admitted that the process forced them to think more deeply about how they felt about dance and why they took it in the first place. The assignment also helped them reset their goals in dance and consider strategies to accomplish them. Wilson's visual component signified his thoughts on males in ballet:[1]

> I made a papier-mâché ballet shoe for this assignment. People don't usually connect ballet shoes with male dancers and I want to make a point that males can do ballet. As a male dance student, I really love doing ballet. It definitely takes a lot of strength for males to do ballet compared to other dance forms. In ballet, males do many lifts and jumps and I think that's way more technical than jazz and modern.

Education theorists including Tom Barone, Elliot Eisner, Ardra Cole, and Gary Knowles have long argued that traditional text-based forms offer limited choices (Barone & Eisner, 1997; Eisner, 1991; Eisner, 2002; Cole & Knowles, 2000). This Dancer & Me assignment invites students to reflect on their own experience in dance and to create something that is non-traditional but meaningful, truthful, and exciting to all. The written component of the Dancer & Me assignment was challenging for many boys; they expressed that although it was difficult to dance physically,

---

1 All names have been changed to protect students' privacy and confidentiality.

it was even more challenging to write about their experience in dance. They had a hard time organizing their thoughts about dance into words. With that said, each boy had a distinct story or message to tell. For the visual component, some participants chose to create a sculpture or compose a rap while others applied the traditional pencil-and-paper strategy to lay out their thoughts. No matter what form they used, the results were fascinating.

The following is an excerpt from a Dancer & Me writing assignment.

> I was extremely intimidated. I found myself surrounded by about forty girls in complete dance attire. I was wearing a T-shirt and some pajama bottoms. I felt and probably looked like a complete idiot. I was sweating crazily and shaking uncontrollably while standing there and thinking about what dance class would be like later on. I would be the only boy taking dance with all girls. Stomping stupidly and tried to catch up with difficult dance routines. Just the thought of it almost made me pee in my pants. In fact, I might have already wet my pants. I was so scared by this that I was seriously considering switching to regular gym where I would have to suffer just one more year.
> — Bruce, "What Am I Doing?"

The Dancer & Me assignment was distributed to male dance students in November, after two months of dance training. It was well received by students, as they saw this assignment as a safe platform for them to express themselves as male dancers. One of the students commented that the assignment was the only place for him to truly voice himself without any other distractions. All grade 9 and 10 male dance students were required to complete this assignment, and all handed in the project. Overall, in the all-boys dance classes, the turn-in rate for this assignment was higher than those for other dance assignments (essay writing and vocabulary review).

Bruce

Bruce was a typical male student who would normally stay away from dance if he were in other schools. Unlike other boys who applied multimedia art forms to make their visual component look fancy, he chose to simply use pencil and paper to sketch out an authentic (and the most creative and self-explanatory) picture. His artwork reflects the image that many males might have in regard to dance. In his text-based component when he was a grade 9 dance student, he confessed his struggles regarding deciding to dance:

I am not going to lie. I am not a dancer, I never have been and I never will be. I have never actually been interested in dance in particular, until I had to choose between dance and gym. Before high school, I've never had to dance and I certainly didn't want to. Choosing dance was a difficult decision because I did not want to be mocked in school, and nicknamed.

As a student who was deeply interested in the arts, Bruce wanted to become either an actor or a painter. He found that selecting Rosedale as his high school was an easy choice, but making a decision to take either gym or dance was a hard one for him. He wrote,

What was I going to do? Look all fruity and girly in a tutu and prance around with girls? I knew I'd be the only guy, and I'd get ridiculed, or even bullied. Was that worth not having to throw a ball eighty thousand yards, just to get some damn respect? Well, in the end it all came down to the pool. If there was anything that I hated as much as sports, it was the swim class! So ultimately, I would rather be made fun of in girly stuff. I chose dance!

Bruce was not alone. Quite a few boys chose dance for the same purpose – to avoid taking gym. Ted Shawn (1960) noted that one might suspect that males abandoned physical education because it was seen as a heterosexual activity and they were homosexual, an observation he made in the early 1900s. My research found that many boys in dance at Rosedale were not homosexual and that the idea they might be thought gay because they danced did not bother them much. Nonetheless, for many, taking dance meant that they could skip gym. Bruce also talked about the first dance experience in his life – a dance placement class in grade 9. According to his description, it was a traumatic and unforgettable experience that he claimed he would remember for the rest of his life. His early struggles in dance were, in many ways, similar or identical to many other male dance students' first dance experience. Bruce's depiction of his first dance experience, Illus. 4.1, shows that he, and perhaps other boys, already had a preconceived notion that dance is for girls and that dance in an educational setting is equivalent to ballet. As I mentioned earlier, the use of ballet as the main form of teaching dance may really be problematic for beginning adolescent boys.

The submitted Dancer & Me assignments had both similarities and differences. Notably, many first-year male dance students used this assignment to talk about their "bumpy ride" towards their first time taking dance. The turning point seemed to come after two months as most of

Illus. 4.1. Bruce's visual component, part one: "What Am I Doing?"

them got used to the physical demands of dance. For males who were taking dance for the second year, assignments usually focused on their positive experience: for example, the change of attitude towards males in dance, benefits from taking dance for a year, and the year-end dance performance. In 2008, after a year of dancing, Bruce presented quite a different Dancer & Me assignment.

In grade 9, Bruce's Dancer & Me assignment looked gloomy and disappointing. However, as time went by, Bruce became increasingly interested in dance. Instead of giving up dance, Bruce excelled. In 2008, Bruce took grade 10 dance, again in the all-boys class. He gained a grade of over 80 per cent in the class by working hard. His progress was so remarkable that one of the dance teachers chose him to dance a lead role for the year-end dance performance. Even more encouraging is that, according to a guidance counsellor in the school, Bruce had already signed up for grade 11 dance.

After taking dance for a while, Bruce's conceptual knowledge of dance, how he saw and thought about it, changed completely. His opinion towards males in dance was completely reformed by the reality of taking dance himself instead of just talking about dance. His active involvement in dance was definitely a major contributor to his positive attitude change. Dance to him meant travelling through time and space on the stage and in the studio. In the 2008 Dancer & Me assignment (Illus. 4.2), Bruce wrote,

> These days my outlook on dance is extremely different from how it began. I am much more physically competent in dancing and I look at dance as more than just an emotional art for girls or even just an alternative to gym class. Dancing with boys makes me stronger. I feel that I am more manly than ever when dancing. I have learned a lot about myself through dance. I don't feel as self-conscious and flimsy as I did before. I am gaining greater self-esteem and confidence. It helps me get anger and fear out by taking my mind off the affecting factors outside of the dance studio. Although I have a very long way to go in terms of skills and technique in dance but I do believe in my ability to become a better dancer!

Michael

Michael had quite a different approach to dance, according to his Dancer & Me assignment. Having dreamed of becoming the "Canadian

Illus. 4.2. Bruce's visual component, part two: "I Am a Man in Ballet"

David Beckham," Michael had worked extremely hard before and after school playing soccer with his neighbours, friends, and teachers ever since he could walk. Before coming to Rosedale, he heard that dance could benefit his skills in soccer, which was a major reason that he chose to take dance:

> I chose dance to help with my future career – soccer. I heard that dance helps the way people play soccer and football. I noticed that I moved more graceful and handle the ball sharply since I took dance. I take it because I want to be a professional soccer player when I grow up.

Researchers including Michael Messner (1990), James Sallis et al. (1997), and Bruce Kidd (1987) have confirmed that dance produces a better quality of training for people involved in sports. Matt Cook (2008), with BBC London, reported that dance, especially ballet, was adopted by many American football teams for their players to gain a greater level of balance, strength, and flexibility. Rachel Howard (2004), a former dance critic with the *San Francisco Examiner*, wrote about the Cleveland Browns football team's successful ballet-football mixed training approach. The team hired Roni Mahler, a ballet teacher, for 12 weeks to train players in ballet technique classes to reduce groin injuries. The result was encouraging: players reported that ballet, especially its turnout method, helped them better control their body and, consequently, decreased the chance of injuries.

In general, adolescent male dance students are less flexible than their female counterparts partially because they started dance training late. For Michael and other male students, flexibility was the most challenging part of dance. The majority of boys in dance showed their resentment towards stretch routines, especially when they had to do peer-stretching, a routine where two students face each other sitting, legs open to each side, while pulling each other with their hands. Despite the painful experience, all the boys in the class recognized that limited flexibility slowed their progress in dance. In regard to flexibility, Michael wrote,

> I think one of the things I have learned in dance is [that] I am not very flexible! As soon as he [dance teacher] says anything to do with stretch, I freak out. I always want to yell and swear when we do peer-stretching. When stretching, I feel that my little "brother" is going to explode. It is awful but I know that is something I definitely have to work on.

Michael was placed in an all-boys dance class but stated that he would not mind being in a mixed-gender dance class. He was one of the few boys who saw almost no difference between an all-boys and a mixed-gender dance class. In fact, he liked to impress girls with his dance skills.

> Having an all-boys dance class doesn't really change my way of seeing dance because I never found dance to be very feminine. Ballet leans a little over to the feminine side. But after taking a month of ballet, I don't think so at all. It doesn't matter to me dancing with an all-boys dance class. I know that being in a girls dance class [mixed-gender dance class] wouldn't be bad, if you know what I mean.

These boys chose dance for various reasons. Some took it for fun and others chose dance because their friends did it and enjoyed it. Whereas, in my view, people in the Gui Zhou province of southern China used dance as a way to look for companions, most boys in dance at Rosedale stated that meeting girls was not their reason for participating in dance.

Like Bruce and other male dance students, Michael talked about his transformation from a potential soccer player looking for supplemental training without any seriousness about dance into an engaged and dedicated male dance student:

> After dancing for a while, I start to like it. No, I begin to love it. My feelings toward dance are positive and I fall in love with dance. I am not that great at it but I still love to move with music just like I have the ball in a soccer field. I may look clumsy compare to how I play soccer but I enjoy moving and thrusting my body in space. That is something I could not do on a soccer field. In dance, I can be anyone.

Michael's visual component (Illus. 4.3) showed a young boy who worked hard in hopes of becoming a strong, flexible, and, to use his word, "attractive" male dancer.

David

As a first-year dance student, David had already expressed his preference for dance. He was born in Costa Rica, and his family and friends were quite involved in the arts when he was a little boy. Whenever there were celebrations such as New Year's Eve or birthday parties, David would

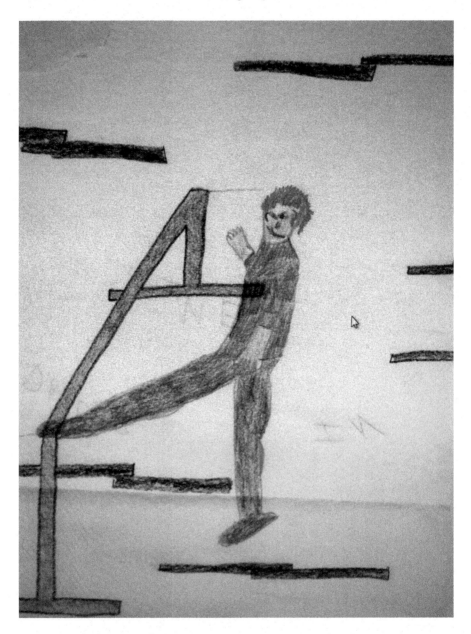

Illus. 4.3. Michael's visual component: "Getting There"

dance with his friends and family members. Dance to him was not anything new, and he felt extremely comfortable doing it. "Not for [a] profession, though," he reiterated. In his written component of the Dancer & Me assignment, he wrote,

> I have always enjoyed the look of dance. Whether it was Michael Jackson doing the moon walk, Mikhail Baryshnikov leaping to great heights or the body isolation performed by mimes, the look of dance has always appealed to me.
>
> I think it is fascinating how dance can be a way of expressing emotion through movement, such as Elvis Presley's anger and sexuality, Fred Astaire's sense of romance and Rudolph Nureyev's passion for life.

After a few months of dance training at Rosedale, David used this assignment to unveil other factors which made him want to take dance seriously. His thoughts on the influence of multimedia on dance were shared among other male dance students:

> I enjoy watching the T.V. show *So You Think You Can Dance Canada* with my family. I love to recognize some of the moves that they do on stage and [I do] in my dance class at Rosedale. Dance is a growing business and may be part of my future career. I have found that dancing offers me the opportunity to be original and a unique young man. Dance challenges me but I love the process [by] which I grow in and through dance.

In his visual component, David drew a male dancer leaping into the air (Illus. 4.4). He explained that he drew that dancer wearing a mask because to him, it shows that "a dancer can be whoever he wants to be when he dances." He further added that the purpose of his artwork is to emphasize his belief in male dancers' strength and masculinity.

While recognizing that he can indeed be whoever he wants when dancing, David himself doesn't embody the confidence that the masked dancer would suggest. As a starting dance student, in class David often wore a big hat or purposely kept his long hair in front of his face. He could be insecure about his personal image or maybe he lacked confidence in dance; during interviews, he repeatedly commented that he would never become a good dancer. He had low self-esteem and a poor concept of himself as a male dancer. He thrived when he received praise and recognition from others. It became clear that such encouragement played a critical role in boosting David's self-esteem. As David received more training in dance, he showed a stronger personality in dance.

Illus. 4.4. David's visual component: "I Can Fly"

Jim

Jim, who was taking dance for the second year, was the only African Canadian student in the class. When friends asked him about his class, they would start with, "How is your hip hop class?" He answered that he actually took modern, ballet, and jazz at Rosedale and there was no hip hop unit whatsoever. Even worse, the person would ask him the same question again and again. He was often frustrated by the assumption of his family and friends that he was inept at dance, especially ballet and modern. In his Dancer & Me assignment, he wrote lyrics and created a rap to represent his ways of seeing dance after two years of taking dance in high school. "Music gets my heart as dance is in my soul." Jim snapped his fingers and mouth-drummed whenever there was a gap in between words. While rapping, he transferred his weight back and forth and moved side to side to fully embody his words, feelings, and thoughts about dance.

George

George created a sculpture for the Dancer & Me assignment (Illus. 4.5). He chose that representation because he liked the idea of making an abstract sculpture to symbolize his different feelings towards dance. Each branch on the sculpture represented different meanings to him. The wind chimes on one of the branches depicted rhythm and musicality. The string of beads draped over the branches symbolized creativity and movement. The wooden hoops and the hands on the sculpture portrayed flexibility and strength. The abstract face on the sculpture was a metaphor for expressive emotion through dancing. In his written component, he talked about his initial thoughts on dance:

> This sculpture represents my mixed feeling towards taking dance. At the beginning of the year, the only reason that I decided to do dance is because I didn't want to do boring gym like everybody else does. Even though I didn't want to do gym I still thought dance would be boring, girly, and stupid.

Tom

Nobody in Tom's family ever thought that he would take dance or actually become interested in dancing. Both of his parents were artists (in acting and music) prior to their current careers (in construction and teaching). As a teenager, he knew the hardships and challenges that an artist's life could bring. As the youngest in the family, Tom was influenced substantially by his brother as he grew up:

> My brother and I got along since I was born. For example, the music I listened to, the activities I got involved with, or the people I hung out with. We both love to attend hardcore and metal concerts. We enjoy being aggressive and loud.

Illus. 4.5. George's visual component: "Versatility"

However, dance became a point of difference between Tom and his brother. His brother, who attended the same arts school and majored in music, went on to pursue a music-related career. Tom chose to take dance and music at the same time at Rosedale:

> Dance is one of the first things I have done that he (my brother) is not in-terested in. Until today, my brother still doesn't quite understand why I took dance in the first place and why I did it again and wanted to take it for the 3rd year consecutively.

Tom's older brother might not know that his younger brother, who shared the same interest in music, gradually developed his "physical voice" in addition to musical talent. While he still played drums, dance became an alternative way for Tom to communicate and express himself. Tom noticed the improvement in his body control and balance after just a year of dance training. Jacques d'Amboise was the founder of the National Dance Institute and a former principal dancer with the New York City Ballet under the directorship of George Balanchine, and he had extensive experience in dance education. Since 1976 he has devoted his life to broadening young children's experience in dance in public schools in the United States. He confirmed that novice dance students usually gain body control and balance first. D'Amboise then suggested that once children gain the body control and balance through dance training, they are more likely to continue dancing (d'Amboise & Seham, 1994). Tom stated that he enjoyed the encouragement that he received in dance class, which matched the peer-appraisal theory presented by dance advocate Jenny Seham. He mentioned that he is thrilled when other students clapped their hands when he did a movement sequence well. That kind of supportive environment made him want to go back to dance classes.

Though disagreeing with his brother, Tom did mention his parents' support:

> I have gotten full support from my parents. They have always encouraged me to do well with whatever subject that I am interested in. Dance is not common in my family but all my family members came to see me dancing at the year-end performance.

In Tom's visual component, he gathered a cluster of pictures to represent his "outside the box" way of thinking about dance (Illus. 4.6). One was a family picture showing the harmony and love he enjoyed at home. In that particular picture, Tom was showing off a newly learned dance sequence in front of his parents. As he danced, his brother took the picture. His brother captured additional photos of a dance move that he learned from an all-boys' dance class. He presented this photo series in a flip book. When a reader flips through the pages quickly, people can actually see him dancing. A childhood dance picture was also included. It was taken when he attended a dance camp at Pegasus Dance Studio 11 years ago at age 3. A close-up of himself was right beside his parents' photo and the original image was at the end.

> My mother had enrolled me in a creative movement camp just to have fun. On the last day of the program we did our "Bumblebee" performance with our parents and I remembered having a big smile on my face the whole

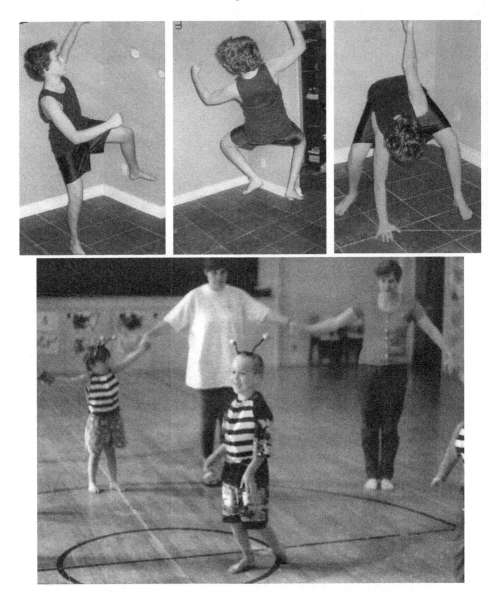

Illus. 4.6. Tom's visual component: Untitled (images scanned from his flip book)

time. We basically did creative dance and mocked the moves that the teacher did in front of us. I would always make my parents laugh. Once I even got the teacher laughing.

When asked why he gave up dance despite the fact that he was good at it, Tom explained that although he enjoyed making his parents laugh, he found that after a while, he was tired of constantly imagining being "trees" or moving like "water" in his classes. It was clear that while young boys enjoy the creative process in making dance, they also need to be technically challenged. A few studies including Lipscomb's (1986) article, "The Trouble with Dance Is Its Name," shared a similar finding that the lack of technical challenge made boys quit dance at early stages. Stinson, Blumenfield-Jones, and van Dyke (1990) did an intensive study on elementary to junior high school students in the United States and discovered that current dance classes offered few choices of styles for boys that would encourage them to continue dancing. They particularly pointed out the adverse effect of introducing or focusing on only creative dance in dance education. They suggested that dance educators should build young people's movement vocabulary first before introducing dance improvisation. There were some dance teachers who assumed that boys could not handle more challenging moves and as a result, boys were asked to create dances on their own. Lita Linzer Schwartz (1977), a prolific author and an expert in children's learning, asserts that when there is no fundamental technique in dance, which is based on rigorous dance training, boys cannot create any meaningful dances. When boys realize what they do is not valued or recognized, they will probably not continue to dance. That might partially explain the lack of a male presence in dance.

Alan

Alan's written component was short, less than a half page. During the interview, he spoke about his first dance experience. It was not him dancing but rather watching his parents dancing at the Toronto Beaches Jazz Festival about 10 years ago. Alan was amazed to see his parents twisting, moving, swinging, smiling, and, best of all, his father throwing Alan's mom over his shoulder. At the time, he was really jealous and wished that he could dance like that. He expressed in his writing,

> It was at that moment [watching his parents dancing on stage], I wanted to learn how to dance. I wanted to be like my dad, a cool dancer who looked so strong and confident while dancing.

Alan's visual component was simply a photo in which his father and mother were dancing in a school gym at the festival. There were a dozen couples dancing on the stage, and his parents were featured in the front line. Alan explained that his father was the one who remembered all the steps and hence was placed in front for others to follow. His movements were clear and precise, and he presented a positive energy to assure his wife, dancing on the right, that everything was under control. "He showed everyone that he was the king on the dance floor," Alan added. His mother, on the other hand, was feeling self-conscious when dancing in front of an audience. She could not even look into Alan's father's eyes because she was afraid that he would do something silly to make her laugh. Alan expressed in his writing that this photo taught him that dance could be a way for people to show emotion, carry on social interactions, and perform for an occasion, and of course, it was a great way to get in shape.

It is widely believed that parents are extremely important in terms of influencing their children's choice of type of education. Many children's first goal is to do what their parents do. Parents become role models in this sense. Alan's first impression of dance was memorable when he saw his father, a grown-up man, dancing with his mother. That incident generated a positive attitude towards dance from a young male perspective.

Kyle

Kyle was the only Chinese Canadian in the focus group. His visual component was a sculpture made of wood (Illus. 4.7). He saw it as a perfect representation of his feelings about dance:

> As a male dance student, it just seems that I can't really see myself as looking graceful. When I dance in ballet, no matter how hard I try to do it correctly, when I look into the mirror it doesn't really look good or like in movies I have seen. I created this wood sculpture to show me as a rigid and ungraceful figure in dance.

In Kyle's written component, he also admitted that like other students in the class, his first dance experience was positive but short. He talked about the first time he saw a dance performance when he was a grade 4 student. His school received free tickets to watch the National Ballet of Canada perform *Nutcracker* at the Hummingbird Centre for the Performing Arts (now the Sony Centre for the Performing Arts). He remembered vividly how those dancers moved on the stage:

Illus. 4.7. Kyle's visual component: "Balance"

The stage was set up beautifully and I found it quite amazing how high many dancers could jump ... Sometimes it seemed like they were gliding or flying on the stage.

An internationally acclaimed British dance choreographer and scholar, Shobana Jeyasingh (n.d.), suggested that all dance pieces represent their makers' life and concerns. In 1998 when Jeyasingh started her own dance company, she spoke about how her study of Indian dance affected her life and her work. Kyle's sculpture functioned in the same way. His visual work spoke about his personal feelings about dance and it also signified many adolescent males' concern about their self-image in dance.

Kyle admitted that the sculpture took much more time than he expected – finding the right piece of wood, gluing the pieces together, balancing the whole object so that it could stand alone. On the way to school, one of the arms fell apart. He had to fix it, but then the head of the sculpture became disconnected while he was fixing the arm. "It was quite a frustrating experience because the sculpture was so fragile." Kyle chuckled. "Well, it was kind of like me in dance. I felt that my body parts were disconnected at times. They [body parts] were difficult to be manipulated while doing everything [watching, dancing, and listening] at the same time!"

The insights gleaned from this assignment are extremely valuable in showing the many dimensions of the boys' beginning experience in dance. The relationship between mind and body is clearly seen, as so many of the boys revealed a change in their thinking towards dance once their bodies got involved. It is noteworthy that for the boys who struggled greatly with dance at the beginning, they struggled with the way they looked – whether they looked competent or not. Later, the increased level of competence and the participation in the all-boys dance class were both important factors for positive attitude changes. It is also important to note that the few boys who did not have a traumatic beginning were those who had a clear purpose in taking dance (e.g., for improving sport skills), not just to avoid gym, and those who had previous exposure to dance through family.

5
Transformation

Many boys talked about their initial dance experience as being fearful and uncomfortable, but interviews conducted after the boys had taken dance for a term showed that they had developed more positive views. Through interviews, the students revealed that they now saw dance as an enriching activity with physical and socio-emotional benefits. They also talked about why they took dance and the sources of influences on their decision to take or continue to take dance. Furthermore, they offered their perspectives on male and female dance teachers and the role that they played at different stages in their dance journey.

After a term (four months), these adolescent males considered dance a fun and joyful activity. They labelled dance as an excellent but rigorous and physically demanding activity. "It is an artistic way to stay fit and healthy," one student stated. Some mentioned that dancing made them a stronger person, while others expressed increased awareness of their food intake. In one of the dance subject units, students had to study what makes a healthy body and food selection. After taking dance for a while, most students indicated that they tended to eat less junk food, instead consuming more nutritious and high-fibre foods.

David suggested,

> Many people in our society are getting really unfit and they kind of loose [lose] everything. Dance is a great way to deal with that problem ... Dance definitely makes me a stronger, healthier, and more disciplined person.

Elizabeth Grosz (1995) in *Space, Time, and Perversion* discussed how people's perception of body capability restricts them from reaching their fullest potential. The involvement of these male students in dance is just an example of how their bodies could exceed their "superficially labeled" limits and help them to achieve more than they had thought possible.

The majority of participants thought dance to be a form of expression. Their description of dance as a *non-verbal means of communication choreographed and arranged in space and time* coincided with the views of many dance educators and researchers. Dance was also viewed as a subject with beneficial effects on other subjects such as music. One student stated, "Dancing is great for my music course. I could not count properly in music but when I was in dance, I had to count the beats while dancing. After a while, I felt that my counting improved in music."

Some young males in this group focused on how dance changed their way of behaving and interacting with others (Illus. 5.1 and 5.2). Most expressed that they were more aware of their posture and alignment while walking and running. They realized that the movements and steps they learned in dance helped them to be more graceful and poised (Illus. 5.3). Two students mentioned that they started to pay attention to the way they moved and acted in drama classes; they both noted that dance would look good on their résumés for future careers. Almost all the participants emphasized that dance made them a more confident person, an idea that was mentioned in Seham's (1997) and Risner's (2009c) work as well as in other studies. In particular, Risner points out that 76 per cent of his study participants (75 males) liked the fact that while dancing, they felt that they could be themselves. Jim noted,

> Right now, I just love doing it [dancing] … I love the fact that I can express my thinking thorough movements. I think it is a personal growth that taking dance brings along with confidence, self-esteem, and a positive self-image.

Carter and Michael shared similar comments:

> In dance, I have to hold myself really well and appear confident. Sometimes I don't know exactly what to do in dance class but I keep trying and trying. (Carter)

> I feel great when I finally learn the movement sequence and dance confidently. I guess that people do that in life, too. (Michael)

During the parent-teacher interviews at Rosedale, many of the students' parents also expressed positive thoughts about how dance affected their children or changes that dance had created for their children.

Illus. 5.1. Boys interact with each other while backstage

Illus. 5.2. Male dance students pay attention to each other's dance exercises

Illus. 5.3. Two male dance students celebrate their successful
"hands-free" lifting

One boy expressed that participating in dance made him feel special.
"It is both artistic and self-rewarding. I think that dance is not only
unique but rather has an important place in society."

When the question was raised of why they took dance, male dance
students at Rosedale responded with different reasons. More than half
ofthem chose dance to avoid taking physical education. When asked why,
many students attributed their decision to the freedom of selecting courses. In the province of Ontario, high school (grade 9 to 12) students can
pick their elective courses. In contrast, students must take physical education courses from junior kindergarten to grade 8, regardless of their
personal preference. Fixed timetables no longer exist in high school because students can select alternative courses. In total, students have to
complete 30 credits (a credit is a full-year course) in order to receive
their high school diploma. Of 30 credits, 18 are compulsory (English,
math, and science) and 12 are elective (physical education or gym, arts,
dance, etc.). Some boys originally took physical education at the beginning of the school year but switched to dance shortly after they found
that dance was equivalent and available in the school. Four boys took
dance as an experimental adventure. One boy in the group confessed

that the reason he took dance was because he thought dance would make him popular among girls. Of course, there were other obscure reasons. For instance, in 2014, five male grade 12 students decided to take dance as a joke but ended up with an unexpected outcome. They all had a positive experience and gained a huge appreciation for dance. These five senior boys eventually became advocates for other males in the school. Two of the five were the president and vice president of the student union, and they frequently regarded dance as one of the most challenging yet rewarding courses that they had taken in school. In all-boys dance classes, the majority of students were in grade 9. Although some of them chose dance over physical education or switched from physical education to dance, this did not mean that they liked dance in the first place. They took dance because it was available in their school. It would probably be a different outcome if the study were held in other schools where dance was not offered.

DeMarco and Sidney (1989) suggested that depending only on physical education to gain adequate physical activity was far from enough. They were not alone. Many physical education theorists in the Western world have voiced concerns over how little exercise students actually receive through regular physical education classes. As seen in Fig. 5.1, more than half of the group said that they took dance to avoid physical education. The original intent for that varied from person to person. Some of them simply did not like sports in general, while others expressed that they were tired of taking gym. After taking dance for a month, many male dance students confessed that dance was actually more physically demanding than gym. Nevertheless, none of the participants gave up dance to switch back to gym.

Two boys who originally took gym for three weeks at the beginning of the school year altered their course selection to take dance instead. They revealed their disappointment in the limited amount of physical activity required in the physical education program. David noted,

> I first took gym class to do exercise but I did not get any because it was just sports and games. I preferred dance because it offered me more physical activities and I could work on specific muscles. Dance class was not only intense but it also required that everyone do it at the same time in the same room. On many occasions during my gym class, I stood at the side of the gym and "observed" others doing things or playing games. My friends who stood by me were usually into their own things, some were chatting while others were on their mobile phones.

Fig. 5.1. Reasons to take dance at high school

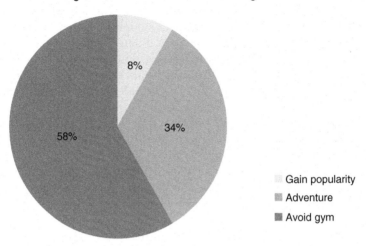

Jim agreed:

> I switched to take dance because I did not feel like taking gym. I felt that if
> I took dance, I would accomplish more workouts.

Male students were more than willing to express their excitement about
taking dance; they were eager to share their workout results.

Some students took dance as an experiment and were later drawn to
it. Tom was a typical example. One day during lunchtime, Tom passed
the big dance studio in the basement and discovered that there was a
hip hop club at the school. The music was loud, and many teenagers
were jumping and shouting in the room. He peeked in and saw some
girls breakdancing in the centre while everyone else was circling around
and clapping. Since he had some krump experience, Tom thought that
he could be the best in the club. He decided to dance in the circle as a
joke, to do something to make others laugh. Although he ran into the
studio to show off his krumping skills, he was soon drawn to a variety of
styles – breakdance, pop, and freestyle – that others were doing. Tom
became a loyal fan of the school's hip hop club after that experience.
He loved being surrounded by other supportive people who were cheering and celebrating dance. He shared his exhilaration when he performed on stage with the hip hop club at Rosedale, which influenced

his decision to sign up for dance again at high school. He said, "[The] African Heritage Assembly with the hip hop club was the turning point for me when I decided that dance was one of the things I wanted to focus on in high school."

His experience performing on stage reinforced a positive attitude towards dance, which subsequently affected his course selection for high school. Originally, he came to Rosedale for music and drama. While he was still interested in music, dance gradually became his favourite subject. He admitted that he experienced "wonder and joy" in dance. Such positive outcomes were shared by many male dance students at the school. During a ballet class in May 2014, one dance student attempted to do a grand jeté, a big jump made from one foot to the other while travelling forward. Being a first-year dance student, he did not have the perfect turnout, nor flexibility and gracefulness. Yet he enjoyed the jump tremendously. "It was like a miracle. I felt that I was flying and turning and flying again until I dropped on the floor." He chuckled.

Some boys who took dance in the previous year decided to take dance again at the grade 10 level. They indicated that the feeling of being a big brother to junior male dance students made them want to dance. George noted,

> We have some grade 9 students in the same class and it is really cool to help them out with difficult steps and movements. I took dance last year and I feel like a role model to coach them on dance moves that I knew.

Adolescents experience many changes both physically and mentally. During this difficult time, they constantly search for role models and seek approval for their own action. Coaching first-year dancers with no experience made these second-year dancers (still relative beginners themselves) feel empowered and hence gain a sense of accomplishment.

A few boys indicated that they ended up taking dance unintentionally. Liam shared his first breakdance incident: "I first started taking dance when my friends kind of forced me to do a hip hop class. It was not serious until I danced for a while. I was more into it when I moved up to a higher level."

Liam is not alone; many well-known dancers started their dance training also by accident. Alvin Ailey, creator of the first American all-black dance company, the Alvin Ailey Dance Company, majored in visual arts at university before he started dance training. Merce Cunningham, the important "chance" inventor whom the *New York Times* claimed

"altered the audience's very perception of what constitutes a dance performance," began to dance to help his dramatic skills (Kisselgoff, 1982).
Cunningham never became an actor; instead he became a soloist in the
Martha Graham Company. He later established his own dance company
in New York – Merce Cunningham Dance Company – which promoted
formless but organic dance structure.

While some stumbled into dance, others wanted to try it because previous physical activities made them think that dance would be easy for
them. David stated,

> I used to be a figure skater for years which meant I kind of had a back-
> ground for dance. I had the flexibility and jumping skills from figure skat-
> ing training and I found it really helpful in dance class.

Likewise, George thought dance would not be difficult because he already had a substantial amount of flexibility, coordination, and strength
from his figure skating training. While recognizing that his previous
training helped him to dance, George later realized that dance used different combinations of muscles and that the flexibility required to dance
well was beyond belief.

Dance also surprised some students. Five grade 12 students, whom I
wrote about previously, had already completed their high school diploma (30 credits). They decided to stay for a fifth year (in Ontario, students can stay in high school for five years even when they have completed
all courses) and chose to take dance together for some fun. "Who cares,
it's just hopping around," one of the boys said before signing up for the
course. It was much more than hopping around, he later admitted.
During the course of the year they were in dance, their attitude towards
dance changed. Their written reflections throughout the year showed
that they began to appreciate dance as an art form and as a curriculum
subject. On the last day of school, one of the students, who was the president of the student union, spoke about his journey in dance while he was
reading the school's daily announcements. Right after "O Canada," the
national anthem, he encouraged all males at Rosedale to take dance. He
spoke about the dance course, teachers, and communal feelings within
the all-boys dance class. He concluded with this statement: "Taking
dance was the best decision I ever made in high school and I wish I did
it earlier." The entire school listened in silence and some applauded at
the end.

Two boys in the study, Robert and Wilson, said that their preschool training in tap dance made them think that they were good dancers (Illus. 5.4). They wanted to become professional dancers at that time. However, as soon as they hit school at the age of six, they stopped dancing. Both had seemingly legitimate excuses for not continuing to dance. Wilson said,

> I previously took one year of tap dancing outside school and I thought it was pretty fun. I stopped taking tap because I guess I have a busier schedule with homework and [other family-related] stuff.

Robert claimed,

> I stopped because there were only four guys in the tap dance company with more than sixty girls.

Their excuses for stopping dance were similar to other boys at Rosedale Heights who took dance at a preschool age. The low ratio of males to females in dance classes resulted in fewer males wanting to take or continue to take dance. This trend continued until a special arrangement was made: creating an all-boys dance class. With that in mind, what influences adolescent males to take dance at Rosedale Heights? Their response: people. According to these boys, there are three key groups of people who affected their decision to take dance in high school – themselves, school staff, and family or friends. Adolescent males who took dance for more than two years stated that teachers and principals were their sources of influence. They further added that performing on stage, in which they experienced a state of optimal enjoyment or flow, a state of complete absorption in dancing, was also a key factor.

Alan chose to take dance in high school on his own. He said that "taking dance seems to be a norm at this school [Rosedale Heights School of the Arts]." To him, it was safe to participate in dance in an arts school because few people would criticize his preference for liking an activity dominated by females. Tom recalled a different impetus for taking dance:

> Nobody. I was a grade 8 student at an inner-city middle school when I got the course selection form for high school. I looked at it and noticed that dance was on the sheet. I decided right there to change things a little bit to get a different flavour in my life.

Illus. 5.4. Robert in preschool tap dance

Both students knew that they were going to take dance in an arts school. To Tom and Alan, the school's focus on the arts created a welcoming environment and hence a safe place for them to pursue something they would not normally do if they were at a regular high school. It is worth mentioning that on the course selection sheet, there was an option for boys to take either an all-boys or a mixed-gender (predominantly girls, without or with only a few boys) dance class. Male students might choose their courses differently if there were only mixed-gender dance classes offered. In this case, both Tom and Alan chose to take dance in an all-boys dance class. It would be interesting to explore whether or not this course availability had any impact on the students' decision to take dance at high school.

School staff, teachers, and principals were a factor for some in deciding to take dance. All of the students in this group implied that the gender of the dance teacher played a major role when they consulted with school staff about making the final decision. Jim articulated,

> I would say that teachers have affected my decision to take dance. It is great to have a teacher [male] whom you could relate to and [that he] has [a] sense of humour ... [In the end] it is me who wants to do it [again] and [because of] the inspiration I got from the dance teacher.

It is widely recognized that one of the most effective strategies to attract males to dance, and to retain them, is to recruit more male dance teachers in the field. British scholar Deirdre Brennan (1996) pointed out that skilled male dance teachers could create a positive experience and thus encourage more males to participate in dance. Rosedale Heights, for example, successfully increased its population of male dance students partially because it had an experienced male dance teacher.

Carter was taking a grade 11 dance major course when this study took place. In the dance major program, he was required to take both ballet and modern technique classes daily. He loved the challenges in dance and the encouragement from others around him.

> I tried it [dance] in grade 10 and I enjoyed it a great deal. My teachers and friends challenged me to take the dance major course and I am really excited to see my progress in dance.

Robert, who was taking dance at the school for the fifth year, used this opportunity to thank his teachers and principals for all their support in his dance training. As a beginner dance student when he first came to Rosedale, Robert never thought that he would choose to pursue dance further. In dance, however, he accomplished more than many people ever expected that he possibly could. After four years of training, both in and outside school, he set his mind to become a professional dancer. Recently, he performed with Opera Atelier, a well-known Canadian performing arts company in Toronto specializing in baroque opera and dance.

> I did get a lot of encouragement from teachers at Rosedale to take dance classes outside the school and get involved in as many things as possible, which turned out to be hugely beneficial to me. The principal [at Rosedale Heights School of the Arts] is really supportive. He is always enthusiastic and excited to hear about something that I am doing. For instance, along with another girl, I was a poster boy for Opera Atelier's 2008 production *Abduction from the Seraglio*. My images are seen on all the pamphlets and programs. He [the principal] took quite a few copies from me and distributed [them] to other teachers and his friends.

Scholars, including Judith Lynne Hanna (1989), have long suggested that people of authority (teachers and a principal in this case) can effectively influence boys' decisions about dancing. Carter was promoted from a dance minor (with dance twice a week) to a dance major program (with dance daily), and Robert had an opportunity to dance with Opera Atelier. It was not easy; Robert and Carter still faced many challenges in dance training, but instead of giving up, they worked harder. It appeared that the boys became more engaged in dance when others recognized their potential and took an interest in their future development. After a year of high school dance training, Robert's ability and determination impressed his teacher so much that the teacher recommended that Robert take professional ballet classes with Opera Atelier (in addition to daytime classes at the National Ballet Company). It was there that Robert became really serious about dancing and wanting to pursue dance as a career option. The artistic director of Opera Atelier, Marshall Pynkoski, an internationally renowned ballet master, recognized Robert's potential and spent extra time to help him realize his dream of becoming a professional dancer. First he took on Robert as a Cooperative Education student so he could observe how ballet and opera production work. Then Pynkoski accepted Robert as an apprentice in his company. Eventually, after a few years of hard work, Robert became one of the dancers in the company. When the students witnessed their improved dance skills and became recognized by others (teachers and principals), they gradually changed their mentality from seeing dance as a joke to considering it a serious subject area.

Most male dance students in the study group preferred males as their dance teachers (Fig. 5.2). The grade 10 students were in their first year of dance, and the grade 11 and 12 boys had at least one year of dance at Rosedale. Two students, one in grade 11 and the other in grade 12, expressed that they did not think gender was an issue in dance teaching. They took extra dance classes outside of the high school with both male and female dance teachers.

Junior male dance students strongly indicated that having a male dance teacher made them feel more comfortable in a dance class. According to them, male dance teachers tended to deliver choreographies that better suit males' needs. In *Dance in the Northern Ireland Physical Education Curriculum*, Deirdre Brennan (1996) recommended the presence of males in physical education, especially when it comes to teaching dance. Instead of starting a dance class with stretching and complex coordination such as upper body isolation, male dance teachers focus on strengthening exercises and jumps, as some boys pointed out. Many others expressed that male dance teachers could relate to them more than female dance educators. Male dance students felt more accomplished and less self-conscious when they had a male dance teacher leading the class.

Male dance students also spoke about female dance teachers. While acknowledging female dance teachers' skills and knowledge in dance, students felt less comfortable when learning choreography. Some students mentioned that in spite of the effort that female dance teachers put into modifying their movements to look more "muscular," the movements still felt unnatural. Jim found it "weird and difficult" to continue dancing with a female dance teacher. He soon transferred from a mixed-gender dance class to an all-boys dance class, which was led by a male dance teacher. Tom expressed similar comments:

> A male dance teacher makes me feel strong and related. He is like a role model to me. If I were having a female teacher, I don't think she would work me as hard. In terms of choreography, I think that female dance teacher would make our dance gentler and I would say girly.

Researchers including Don Mirault (2000) and Margaret Talbot (1993) have long advocated for a male presence in dance education. They noted the significance of having male dance teachers. Talbot (1993) stated that

Fig. 5.2. Preference for male or female dance teachers

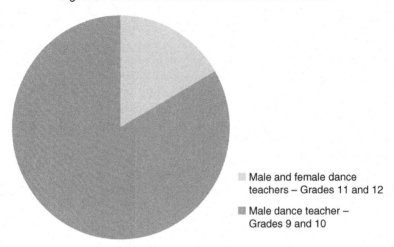

Male and female dance
teachers – Grades 11 and 12

Male dance teacher –
Grades 9 and 10

gender influence is important in attracting and keeping males in dance, whereas other scholars including Amanda Berger (2003), Joseph Grady (2002), Mary Benoit (2000), John Crawford (1994), and Day Bev (2001) argued that teaching methods are more critical. Deirdre Brennan (1996), Karen Bond (1994), and Michael Gard (2001) further suggested that these methods require frequent modifications to maximize success for boys. In other words, dance educators constantly need to evaluate and re-evaluate their teaching methods in light of how male dance students learn.

Two senior dance students taking classes both inside and outside of school had different opinions. They had each had numerous dance teachers, female and male, in the past and at present. Both respected their dance teachers as experts in the field with different approaches to help them become stronger dancers. At this stage, gender had less impact on their learning as a dancer. Robert said,

> They are both beneficial. They are good teachers as long as they know how to teach different genders and they know how they differ [from one to another]. Some teachers who really pushed me happen to be females. They kind of break me apart and put me back together. They make my legs wobble when I walk away from the class.

Carter, the other senior dance student, also stated that there was little difference in learning dance from either male or female teachers. However, he admitted that male teachers tended to focus on upper body training, which let them feel more in control while dancing. It's worth mentioning that both senior students admitted that it was easier to connect with male dance teachers, especially when they had just started to take dance. As Jim, a first-year dancer, pointed out, "He [the male dance teacher] becomes a direct role model and my personal goal. It's like something I look up to and to use to motivate my own drive."

Family and friends play important roles in affecting young males' decisions about course selections. Through interviews, I found that many students' parents had deliberately sent their sons to attend Rosedale Heights School of the Arts. Although many parents were not employed in the arts or related careers, they were involved in arts-related activities or previously employed in the arts. These boys recognized their parents as being interested in the arts or at least not against them. Seven out of 12 participants revealed that they had one or more family members who had an experience in theatre, dance, music, or visual arts at different stages of their life. The other five boys did not talk about their family's involvement in the arts. David talked about his parents' previous arts-related experience as a main factor in his decision to take dance. Before course selection, his parents reminded him that he had taken gym for all of his previous school years. They suggested that it might be time to try something new:

My parents had the biggest influence on me. They thought it would be great for me to take dance. Both of my parents were very involved in the arts until they were in their late 20s. My mother likes dancing and stuff like that.

Interestingly, he was the only one in this interview who talked about the influences of other male dancers whom he watched on TV shows. He described those male dancers as role models in his life:

Media created a lot of influence on me as well. *So You Think You Can Dance Canada* put on all types of dance and many males are in it. I was always eager and excited to watch that show. Sometimes I would try something they did on my own.

A few boys in this group claimed that their parents were liberal in terms of giving them freedom to choose their courses in high school. When they were not sure whether to take gym or dance, parents casually suggested dance because dance was a special program at Rosedale and not offered at every high school. These young males admitted that their friends who took dance also influenced them in that direction. Liam shared a story about how his mom persuaded him to take dance seriously:

> My mother is being too supportive that she even takes class at the place where I used to dance. She is not a dancer as she used to be a figure skater when she was little. I think that she tries to convince me that if she can do it, so can I.

The majority of these students' parents were not involved in the arts at the time the interviews took place. However, their previous experience in the arts or dance directly or indirectly affected their son's choice to take dance in high school. Some parents said that they took dance when they were young but were either told not to continue by their own parents or were persuaded or even pressured to stop dancing because their friends were not dancing. Some were concerned about the legitimacy of dance as a career option. One mother confessed that she wanted her son to take dance because she could not realize her own dream of dancing when she was little. She was forced to quit dance before university, even though she received a scholarship for a prestigious dance program. Needless to say, these parents were advocates for the arts; otherwise they wouldn't have signed the admission letter to allow their son to go to an arts school.

Almost all the participants in this study confirmed that their families had supported their decision to take dance in high school. Some indicated family had more influence while others claimed less. Only one boy indicated that he had trouble explaining his rationale for taking dance to some of his family members.

As the only African Canadian in the study, Jim complained about mixed views that he received from his family members:

> Some [family members] are against my decision to take dance. They suggest that I might as well take gym. Others in my family actually supported my decision to take dance. It was like half-half and I was confused about their willingness of whether or not they supported me to take dance in high school.

Kyle did not expect to take dance in high school. However, he assumed that his parents supported him because his mom signed him up for dance without his consent. Meanwhile, he said that his mother promised him he could drop the course if he did not like it. His story coincided with my own personal story in which my parents ordered me to take dance. The difference was his parents would have allowed him to drop out if he did not like it, whereas I did not have that choice.

The students listed different kinds of support that they received from their family. Alan, a multiracial male dance student of Ukrainian and Southeast Asian Indian descent, boldly guessed that it was his father's inability to dance that made him support his son's choice to dance in high school. Alan joked,

> My father probably has two left feet and he is not even musical. He had a hard time chasing my mom, a Ukrainian girl, who was good at folk dance. On their wedding day, they were supposed to present their first dance in front of hundreds of guests. My father was so nervous that he forgot all his steps. He stumbled all over the place and made everyone in the room laugh their heads off.

It was assumed that Alan's father, of Indian descent, knew how to dance. But when he migrated to Canada with his parents, Alan's grandparents, he was only an infant and never had the chance to take dance in his life. Like many others of Indian descent in Canada, he devoted all his time to academic subjects such as math and science. Now a high-profile consultant at IBM, Alan's father most likely realized how much he had missed in his childhood. His lack of knowledge in dance possibly resulted in his recommending that Alan take dance in high school.

Several boys who took dance for a second year admitted that their involvement in the school productions made their family look at dance seriously. Their parents were so stunned and impressed by the year-end dance performance that they came to volunteer for the following year's dance production. One parent worked backstage ironing and assisting with make-up while others spent a few nights at the school building props for the dance show. George commented,

> My mother said that she was going to volunteer at the dance production. At first, I thought that she was joking. She drove me to the school on the dance night and headed right to her duty, ironing dance costumes. She was so diligent with her volunteering position that she forgot to take my dinner out from the car. I had to remind her and get the dinner on my own because she was that busy. I thought that she was crazy but later I changed my mind.

She did it for me, for the dance program and for the school. Her involvement made me want to do better in dance and that [is] probably the reason that I am still in dance now.

Other parents showed their support in different ways. Tom's parents would push away the furniture in the living room to give him space to practise dance movements. Seeing their son's dance routines, both of them agreed that dance was much more physically demanding than they had expected.

John Dewey (2007) suggested that one's past could greatly affect his/her present. It was intriguing to see how a professional dancer within a family affected another family member's thinking on dance. Carter talked about his mom, who used to be a ballerina in the New York City Ballet. His mother's earlier profession and the way she looked at dance effectively changed his father's mind about paying for dance lessons for Carter outside of school. His father's decision might have been different if Carter's mother had never danced before. A person who has a strong interest in a certain subject can easily sway another person's mind. In this case, Carter's father's support of his son in taking dance was influenced by his mother's previous experience in dance.

A number of the students shared similar scenarios in which their mothers acted as cheerleaders for dance in the house. These mothers followed *So You Think You Can Dance* and *Dancing with the Stars* on TV diligently, and they even took dance classes as a hobby. "My mom loves dancing so much and she would show me what she learned from the dance studio. That was a bit too much," Liam said, raising his eyebrows. "The whole family came to see my performance, though, which was really nice," he added. David's parents suggested that taking dance might open new doors for him. His dad was a popular student who was really good at all sports when he attended high school in Mississauga, Ontario. He told David,

> The whole of sports is great, but it would be even better if you open to new ideas such as dance and other forms of arts. You don't know what will end up being useful. I was a star in sports but I did not become a professional in that business. However, I learned so much in sports in terms of working together with others and supporting each other in difficult times. I assume that dance would be the same if not more. You should dance now when you can because I cannot.

Whether it has to do with parental support or not, many dance educators interviewed for this study agreed that the number of males participating in dance had increased in recent years. From Ted Shawn's first all-male dance company to the Jacob's Pillow Dance Festival, from *Billy Elliot* to *So You Think You Can Dance*, it has become harder for people to ignore the visual appearance of male dancers. Some parents in this study considered dance as a way to become an instant celebrity, while others looked at dance more realistically and logically.

On the other hand, not all students focused on the physical aspects of dance. Wilson, for instance, used "dance training" as an excuse to get something he desired – a Nintendo Wii console. Wilson's parents supported him to the extent that they bought him a Wii Fit game at his request to increase his flexibility and strength in dance, although Wilson admitted that he spent most of the time on Mario games. "It really worked," he whispered.

Robert had mixed feelings about his mother's support. He assumed that his mother did not fully understand what it took to be a professional dancer and was curious if his mother would still support him if she knew how much effort it really took to become a professional dancer.

> She [my mom] does not fully understand how much work it takes and how tiring it can be. After school and dance training, I came home really late at night. She asks me to do more things when the only thing I could do is to go to bed ... I find it really hard to make my own parents understand what it takes to be a professional dancer.

Paul Willis (1981) discussed in his book how working-class children get working-class jobs. Many parents want to see their children pursuing the same or similar careers as their own, partially because of familiarity or their own fear of experimenting with something "unsafe." For example, Liam, who stumbled into dance by accident, claimed that his mom had tried to convince him to do figure skating since she did it when she was young. It did not work. After a few years of high school dance training, Liam became really serious about pursuing dance as his future career. In addition to high school dance courses, Liam took dance classes six days a week outside the school. He decided to audition for the Juilliard School in New York after high school. Liam's mother, who was not sure about her son's choice of dance at first, was moved by his dedication and determination. After some thoughtful conversations, Liam convinced his mother in this matter and she eventually supported her son in pursuing dance at the post-secondary level. While conflicts can exist between parents and adolescent male dance students, respectful and meaningful communication is strongly recommended. In Robert's case, his mother might understand better if Robert took her to observe one of his ballet classes or rehearsals and explained to her the rigorous physical training and the time-consuming process required to become a professional dancer.

In addition to teachers and parents, friends of these adolescent males also had an impact on their decision to take dance. This study showed that there were two different kinds of friendships: previous (elementary/family) and present (secondary). Junior high school males in this study (grade 9 and 10) admitted that they were influenced by friends who were a year or two older and had attended the same junior high school. Older students in dance also became role models for younger students in elementary schools during visiting performances. Some boys indicated that their family members' involvement in dance got them interested in trying out dance. That included their sisters, brothers, cousins, and other relatives. Another kind of friendship was the present friendship, when boys bonded together while taking dance. These became quite influential, as boys who progressed well in groups were more inclined to take dance again in high school, bolstered by their newly established friendships in dance.

Interacting with other peers in the school served as another main reason for adolescent males to opt for dance. These dance-related conversations usually took place during lunchtime and after school. Two students in the focus group acknowledged that casual talks among friends swayed their original thoughts on course selection. They chose dance over other subjects they originally thought they would take. In fact, more than half of the participants admitted that their primary conception of male dancers had been fundamentally changed after interacting with friends. As a result, they too decided to participate in dance, as it no longer was associated with abnormal or female-only activity.

The students expressed that they received mixed responses from friends, some of whom expressed some support for or acceptance of their involvement in dance. Still, they admitted that there were misunderstandings and biases among their non-dance friends. These adolescent male dance students could be organized into four groups based on the responses of their friends – partial acceptance, full acceptance, self-acceptance, and beyond acceptance (those who serve as role models); see Fig. 5.3.

Several boys were in the partial acceptance group. All of them expressed that they were supported by their friends at Rosedale, where they took dance alongside academic subjects. However, when they talked

Fig. 5.3. Views on dance

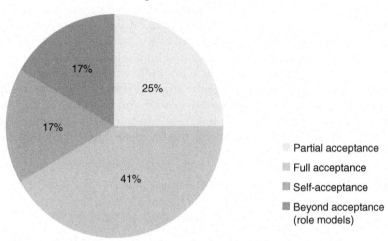

about their dance experience to friends outside school, they received less positive remarks. Jim mentioned that his friends laughed at his preference for dance in high school. They were surprised to hear that Jim did not take gym but dance. "Don't you have physical education?" they asked. Jim would defend himself by saying, "Dance is my physical education." Then Jim went on to describe how intense and rigorous his dance class is, which surprised many of his friends, who thought that dance was just "prancing around with beautiful girls." David and Liam shared similar experiences in which their outside school friends deemed them as unmacho and unfit men because they took dance. Liam felt so insecure that he would tell his friends that he was only in the hip hop club. He argued that "it [hip hop] is extremely popular among teenagers and there is nothing bad about that." Michael Gard (2003b) presented similar findings on males' attitudes towards sports and popular dance forms. David shared his friends' unpleasant but stereotypical comment on dance, which might represent the majority of people's view on males in dance:

> My old friends from my former school [Catholic school] respond very differently. They think that only girls should dance. They accept skating because they can relate it to hockey, which is a man thing. They would say to me like: "Wow, dance, that's weird."

The majority of the adolescent male dance students in this study said that their friends fully accepted their involvement in dance at high school. It was noticeable that their remarks on this topic tended to be short and succinct. Usually it was described as "that's cool," "that's neat," or "it's fascinating that you take dance in high school." All of them had friends both inside and outside the school who were actively involved in dance or in other arts subjects. These students thrived in a comfortable environment in which they were supported and accepted, and dance seemed to be a norm to them and those around them. Carter considered himself fortunate to be one of the few male dancers, treasures in this profession:

> None of my [male] friends has done anything like that [dance] before. They think it is really neat to know how to dance. They know that not many boys are in dance and I am one of the few. They are happy that they have a male dancer friend.

Their participation in dance was not only accepted but also celebrated. While dancing, they established a sense of belonging and identity and they felt comfortable among others in high school. They were confident, not necessarily because they were good dancers but because they valued what they did in class and they enjoyed their time dancing.

With more dance training under their belt, senior students, those who had taken dance for two years or more, expressed their confidence in dance. They took dance seriously and rejected the stereotypical views that males should not dance. Robert explained that since he was a senior dance student (it was his fifth year in dance), friends saw him as a principal dancer belonging to some kind of dance company. Years of dance training made him stand out even when he wasn't dancing. He stood up taller, walked with confidence, and delivered his other course presentations with many body gestures. Robert said, "My friends look at me as more of a dancer rather than a regular high school kid because I am so involved in dance performances both inside and outside the school."

Nonetheless, he gave credit to the fact that he was in an arts school where the majority of students were enthusiastic about arts. "If I were in a different school, I don't think it would be the same," he concluded. Although his words implied that males in an arts school are more likely to take dance than those attending regular high schools, this is not entirely accurate. At the Etobicoke School of the Arts (ESA), a much older and more established arts school in Toronto, founded in 1981, there were far fewer boys taking dance than there were at Rosedale. A similar result was found at Earl Haig Secondary School, which has offered its well-known Claude Watson Arts Program since 1982. Were boys afraid of taking dance, even when they attended an arts school? That would contradict Robert's opinion. While collecting data, I also spoke to several dance educators who worked in regular high schools in Toronto that offered dance courses. Many of these teachers noted similar proportions of male and female dance students. A few dance teachers admitted that their dance program did not have any males. What happened in the dance program at Rosedale? How did it attract, maintain, and grow its male dance population? One finding stood out from this research: all-boys dance classes.

Rosedale offered all-boys dance classes. Etobicoke School of the Arts, Earl Haig's Claude Watson Arts Program, and other regular high schools did not have such classes. Rosedale had many more boys taking dance in junior grades and continuing to take dance in the senior grades than the other schools. This implied that dance could be attractive to junior high school students when there was a safe and nurturing environment – such as an all-boys dance class. It was evident that being in an arts school alone did not mean that boys would feel safe and hence more willingly take dance. This could also be interpreted to mean that being in an arts school was not enough to attract and keep males in dance. Something extraordinary had to be done. Creating an all-boys dance class was one of the effective solutions to attract more males to take dance.

Tom was a good example. He took dance in an all-boys dance class for the second year straight. He felt proud of himself and was confident about his choice to take dance again. He stated,

> I don't like people who disrespect my decision to take dance or any other subjects I take at the school. I decide not to be around those people. I like dance and music in general. I see no point to include those people who don't enjoy what I like in my life.

Like Tom, other adolescent male students justify their taking dance by talking about doing it for enjoyment, having witnessed and experienced positive outcomes both physically and mentally. These students deliberately choose to take dance again, but not for the purpose of forming alliances with other students with whom they are comfortable and familiar. They simply want to experience again what they enjoyed the most, both on stage and in the studio.

Two boys expressed that they considered themselves role models in high school. Both boys were popular in school and both were fully supported by their family and friends regarding taking dance. They loved the physical challenge and artistic approach in and through dance and were eager to share their positive experiences in dance with others. In return, they both inspired a couple of other male students who were not sure about dance to take dance in high school.

David suspected that the low interest among males was due to a misunderstanding. He assumed that if more males participated in dance, it would become pointless to call anyone names such as "gay" or "girly man." David further unfolded his personal experience with other male students:

> Everyone around me [students at Rosedale] thinks it is a cool idea to take dance. They are really supportive and saw me as big brothers in dance ... One of my friends, Ken, did not take dance at the beginning but saw the amount of work I put into dance. He switched to dance and since then, have enjoyed it quite a bit. There is no downside if everyone does it [dance]. But if only one person does it, he can be singled out.

Gender identity is well established here, as dance has become increasingly viewed as a normal activity to a large number of male participants. They see movements as organic and foundational to represent the whole body and mind. Dance as a subject is subsequently reinforced in all social interactions, in which male dance students encourage other males to participate in dance. There is no gender discrimination against male dancers in any form; instead, dance is celebrated and promoted among adolescent male students. Students in this safe and comfortable environment can freely enjoy taking dance with little or no social repercussions.

Only two students in the study indicated that they experienced certain forms of social repercussions. The majority of students either said "not at all" on the survey or stated that their friends simply accepted the fact that they took dance in high school. Students also pointed out that their friends' responses varied; some of their friends expressed less welcoming comments, while others thought taking dance was an interesting adventure.

The majority of students in this study stated that they had never experienced any negative social repercussions. Half of this group were students who were taking dance for the first year. Because this interview took place early in the school year, many of them had not had a chance to inform others about their involvement in dance.

For those who had taken dance for a year or more, they replied with similar responses such as "not really. Nobody has ever criticized or judged my decision to take dance. None of my friends or family members thinks it is abnormal for me to take dance as they are quite open to it." Three students did not pay too much attention to how others felt about their involvement in dance. Jim stated, "It is really just that they accept it. It is a high school elective course and they cannot do anything about it. Well, taking dance in high school for free and to get a credit. What a luxury!" Carter assumed that it could have been different if he were in a non-arts-based school, but so far nobody had ever looked down on him because he took dance.

Alan and David had a slightly different experience. They both expressed that their friends (outside Rosedale) thought dance was an unfit subject for them to take in high school. "If you take dance, you are strange," one of David's friends said. However, "it did not happen a lot as most of my friends supported me for taking dance," David added. Alan's friends also made less positive remarks.

> Wow, that's amazing or that is fascinating. Some would giggle when they comment. I don't think that they were shocked. I think that they were more surprised because I am a clumsy person. I don't look like someone whom they think would normally take dance.

He laughed at that.

Robert and Liam were the only two students who revealed that they had experienced some form of social repercussions. Liam said,

> When I told my old friends outside of the school that I am taking ballet, they were saying what the f——. They started to laugh at me. I know that they have no idea of what I was talking about it because they had never experienced ballet themselves.

Liam was the only one who had moved from a sports-oriented school to Rosedale for the arts. Most of his friends went on to high schools that focused on physical education and other competitive activities. On many occasions, he almost had to argue with his former friends about how much dance required both physically and mentally. He further stated,

I really liked ballet. I did not feel there is anything wrong with it. I did not let their comments/attitudes get to me. I personally enjoyed it dearly and to me that matters the most. All my male friends are playing sports. They quickly stopped when they noticed that I was not bothered at all. I actually told them that ballet is one of the hardest dance styles ever. I even tell my friends that ballet is harder than all the sports that I have played in the past. I challenge my friends to take ballet but none of them have the courage to do that. It is funny because I can do the sports they are doing and they cannot do "ballet" as I do. Once they realize that, they have no excuse to bother me.

Some educators – including Sarah Stevens, an assistant coach of the Iowa State University's Dance Team, and Professor Irene Glaister from Bedford Physical Education, United Kingdom – are advocates of dance being under the physical education curriculum (Glaister, 1987; Stevens, 1992). Many deem it unproblematic for physical education teachers to deliver dance lessons. In reality, that is not the case. According to students who had taken physical education courses previously and then took dance at high school, dance should be separated from physical education. "They [physical education teachers] simply would not teach dance," one student said. Liam spent three years in a junior high school that focuses on sports. One would assume that he must have had certain forms of dance or movement-based training, or at least that students in that school would not look down on people who take dance. In contrast, Liam claims that there was no dance component in his sports-focused school. To make it worse, nobody in the school, including teachers and students, seemed to have a problem with the fact that dance was not offered. Why did teachers not deliver some kind of dance component in their well-established physical education program? It might be due to the teachers' lack of experience in dance, as some educators and scholars have suggested. Bleakley and Brennan (2008) state in their research that dance is generally not valued in school, and therefore, students rarely have any opportunity to learn dance. Michael Gard (2008) further points out that male students assume that only girls dance; dance is inevitably deemed as a "sissy" or "taboo" activity to males.

Robert brought up the gender imbalance issues in dance. He admitted that while juggling his busy ballet training schedule, both in and outside school, he felt lonely sometimes. He shared his thoughts with a serious tone:

The main one [issue] would be that dance is about 97% girls. I have some guy friends but I don't have any strong base guy friends. I find that frustrating. That means I am always hanging around with girls most of the time, which is nice at times. I have a really hard time making good friends who are both in ballet and whom I want to hang out with. Another thing is that I devote most of my personal time to train myself in ballet. That means I have little time to enjoy other teenagers' activities [parties, clubs, movies, etc.].

Nonetheless, Robert emphasized that he fully understood that it was his choice to stay in dance. He knew that he was considered to be a late starter. Robert began to take ballet classes seriously when he was about 16 years old with little dance background, compared to many others who started dance when they were 6. "I got a lot to catch up on." Robert smiled and shrugged his shoulder. Robert's comment on the number of males and females in dance is no surprise. Both scholarly studies and reality show the evidence of few males in dance. Although males enter dance for different purposes, there is no doubt that it takes a lot of determination and perseverance for males to stay in dance. But how far in the future do they see themselves in dance?

When participants were asked if taking dance would or would not help them in the future, all replies were positive. All responses addressed the logical aspects, including benefiting health, having it as a hobby, and strengthening body posture. Out of all 12 participants, only a few considered dance as a career option.

Three participants, all taking dance for the second year, admitted that dance had become a new hobby for them. They were fascinated to explore this new physical activity with great interest. While dancing, one boy felt that he could do anything he wanted. He forgot about where he came from and who he was and could enjoy the moment being in dance, an emotional state shared by students with more dance experience, usually a year or more. Michael said, "I see dance as a hobby. I love dancing. Of course, when I grow older, I could look more than cool and funny by doing a ballet turn. I think people would be jealous." In terms of jealousy, Liam added, "Whenever I go out to a club, I find that knowing how to dance is pretty useful. A sense of movement and being able to dance makes me socially popular. It makes me look more impressive. People, especially girls, respect me a lot more when they see me dancing."

The longer students took dance, the more positive factors they experienced from dancing. All the adolescent males in the study expressed that dance was not only a hobby or a way to stay healthy. Dance became part of their life, though they did not begin dance training until high school. One student noted, "Scientifically dancing pumps more blood to a person's brain and supplies more oxygen ... in return it [dance] makes that person's brain to work more efficiently."

Robert was one of the two students who wanted to pursue dance professionally. With five years of dance training, both within and outside of high school, he was excited and anxious about his future plans in dance. To be better equipped, Robert also took drama and music at school. He stated,

> I definitely consider dancing as a profession for me. It is already part of me at present ... For that goal, I am willing to dance in musical theatre, work as a choreographer and director and to do other things in order to survive in the field. To scale back, my immediate goal is to become a dancer at the moment.

Meanwhile, Robert admitted that he was aware that a dance career could be short compared to other options. That was exactly the reason he wanted to be a professional dancer now, or hopefully soon. As a young adult, he did not want to have regrets in his life because he did not try. He wanted to do it now instead of postponing it to another time, which meant it might never happen.

At present, Robert is one of the most celebrated male dancers performing with Opera Atelier in Toronto. His performances have been reviewed by the *New York Times*, the *Globe and Mail*, and the *Toronto Star*. In 2012, he toured with the company to France and the United States. In 2013, he danced in Opera Atelier's newest production, *Magic Flute*, which had been performed in Austria and other east European countries before its Toronto premier. When asked if he regretted his decision to become a professional dancer, he laughed and stated, "I could hardly imagine what dance has done for me as an individual. Looking at my [high school] classmates who have graduated from university and [are] still trying to figure out what to do, I guess that I am ahead of the game. I feel fortunate that I continued in dance."

Three students – Michael, Carter, and Liam – were uncertain at one point about what to do with dance in the future. All three students had taken dance at Rosedale consecutively for three years. Michael took dance at Rosedale only, whereas Carter and Liam also did extra dance classes outside the school. With less dance training, Michael was uncertain about the option of dancing in the future:

I have thought about it. I have to admit that I don't see myself as a dancer, yet. It depends on what is going on. I don't know ... I know that I am not quite good enough for that just yet. I might be and I could be but I don't know how I could get there at this point.

Both Carter and Liam were somewhat inclined to opt for dance as a career but they, too, saw dance as a "risky" profession. Carter, whose mother used to be a professional dancer, was taken aback by seeing her suffering from post-dance-career consequences:

I thought about it. However, it is really hard to do it as a profession because it is really a short career. I know that my mom really enjoyed it when she did it. Now, she sort of regrets it because the injuries that she ends up with after quitting dance. Now she has foot and back problems from her dancing career.

Regardless, Carter believed that training in dance would help him in succeeding in any field that he might pursue later in his life. On that note, Liam juggles two potential careers that he might be interested in – music and dance:

I see two paths in my life. I could continue with my music and dance just as a hobby and get a regular job ... I could become a versatile dancer who could dance for commercials and could just go and may enter a tournament for breakdance if I ever got good at that. Or, I may choose to do ballet, which is something I like less than breakdance. It is still dancing and I believe that I would probably be happy to do something I really like.

Seven participants, all having taken dance for two years or less, rejected dance as a career option in the future. Students who had just begun dancing at Rosedale (four months at this point) were reluctant to even talk about dance as an option. David, a first-year dance student, suggested that taking dance would benefit his acting career (similar to Merce Cunningham, who ended up switching from pursuing drama to dance). Other students, including David, expressed that they would continue dancing. Jim noted,

For me, dance will not be my profession because I want to be a computer programmer. I see dance as a hobby. I love dancing. I would take dance workshops or attend dance shows in the future when I grow older ... Right now, I just love doing it.

Tom and George both attempted to figure out their potential career paths, which were all considered to be "not reliable." Tom said,

> Being in any form of arts I know is not a reliable career. I see some reality shows talking about how dancers have a fantastic time partying in Los Angeles and New York. While seeing they are living in it, I know that it is not common in real life. I don't really see it as a career at this point but a fantasy. I have always wanted to take music as a career but there again not very reliable. At this point, I don't really know what I want to do yet.

Data showed that the more dance training students received, the more likely they were to be interested in taking dance classes in the future. The less training they had in dance, the less likely they were to be serious about taking more dance training and, as a result, the less likely they were to consider becoming a dancer in the future. Three years seemed to be the turning point when adolescent males' attitude towards taking dance shifted from it being a hobby or a health-benefiting activity to being recognized as a legitimate career option. More boys participating in dance cultivates a safe environment, in which taking dance is deemed normal. It becomes even more evident when this takes place in an arts-focused school.

The adolescent male dance students conveyed that, while there might have been different reasons for them to take dance, people close to them played an important role in their choice. For boys, receiving support from peers, teachers, and family members is one effective way to increase the male presence in dance. This finding confirms Risner's (2009c) study about the importance of alliance (other males in dance) and family members who sincerely care and are supportive. Having male teachers at the beginning also created a sense of security. Their exposure to dance, the duration of dance training, and performance had an impact on how they viewed dance from then on. It is noteworthy that increased competence and public acknowledgment led to boys' consideration of pursuing dance professionally. As Alan said,

> In the future, I will continue to dance, maybe not as a profession. I am not too clear at this point. I know I am heading to university but surely not for mathematics. I am eliminating options instead of finding one thing.

6
Invisible Barriers

In this chapter, young boys at Rosedale reveal their mindsets concerning the public, stereotypes, and the prospects for males in dance. After spending almost a year in dance classes, the majority of the students still did not want to share their experience in dance, for various reasons. Among them was the fear of being laughed at because they danced. Only a few boys would admit to "others" about their involvement in dance without hesitation. These "others" refer to those who were not familiar with the participants. More importantly, these male dance students offer their thoughts and recommendations on how to deal with some of the barriers and share their words of encouragement.

Interviews with adolescent males in dance showed an interesting trend: junior dance students seemed to be less willing to reveal their participation in dance to others. In contrast, seniors, who had taken dance for two years or more, were fine when talking about their involvement in dance. It is worth pointing out that these boys would first tell others that they were in an arts school before letting them know their dance experience. They would purposely emphasize the fact that they also took general high school courses such as math and English.

Those who had taken dance for a year or less preferred not to disclose anything about their dance class until they got to know more about their new friends. Until then, they would rather talk about something else. When they knew each other more, they would tell them that they were in an arts high school and that they were taking boys' dance as well as other subjects. They would emphasize that they were in "all-boys" dance classes, seeming to aim at forming some level of mutual understanding or alliance, as Anna Aalten (1997), of the University of Amsterdam, suggested in "Performing the Body, Creating Culture." Gard and Meyenn

(2000) also presented a similar argument in their study on boys' preference for physical activities. While talking with adolescent males in dance,
I found that they hoped others (those in dance and those not) would not
see them as abnormal because they danced. David stated,

> I am going to an arts school and I am taking all-boys dance, drama, and vi-
> sual arts. I say boys dance because they [other people] are always curious
> about it and most definitely they would ask questions around it ... I say it
> first so that they might not ask further questions.

Kyle, who was in his first year of taking dance, shared similar comments. He also talked about the uniqueness of an all-boys dance class:

> Drama, dance, and vocal, I will not mention about other academic courses
> because everyone does that. I like dance a lot because it's all guys. It is a re-
> ally comfortable environment. I feel that it [all-boys dance class] is created
> for males' need and I learn a lot of muscular moves.

In contrast, Carter, who had taken dance for more than two years, was
much more comfortable and confident when discussing his course selections with any new friends in public:

> I would answer that I am going to an arts school with a focus on dance. On
> top of that, I am taking all the regular high school courses ... I am doing a
> dance major course that requires me to take ballet and modern on a daily
> basis.

Robert, who had taken dance for more than four years, further stated,

> I would respond that I take the academic courses such as math and science
> ... I would really emphasize the fact that I am taking multiple artistic cours-
> es such as musical theatre and dance. Meanwhile, I also do extra training in
> ballet outside school.

Regardless of whether or not these adolescent males saw dance as a
career option, it seemed that all boys felt the need to justify their choice
of taking dance to people they didn't know well, emphasizing either
that they took other academic subjects as well or that they were in an
all-boys dance class. Since these responses were formulated using a hy-
pothetical situation, they show that there was indeed a perception for

these adolescent males that the public did not consider dance a legitimate avenue of study for males. This thinking could create an invisible barrier for these males in dance and perhaps, when further confirmed by the public, whether intentionally or unintentionally, would then strengthen their beliefs that dance should not be pursued by males.

Michael and George's inner struggles provide a more detailed example of the internal barriers that adolescent males can experience. While Michael enjoyed dancing, he often suspected that others were talking about or judging his ability, or, according to him, his "inability" to dance:

> I scare myself a lot by holding it back. I am still a bit self-conscious when dancing in front of people. I know [that] it is just a little worm inside my body that bugs me. It is not because I am a boy and I take dance. I believe that I am born to be a dancer although I am not one, just yet. I am working on it.

As a student who had gymnastics training at a young age, George thought dance would be much easier for him. It was not at all.

> My biggest challenge was making the decision to stay or go. I really did not want to take gym at that time but I was having such a tough time that I wanted to quit dance. I found it was hard to keep up with others in the class.

Unlike Michael and George, who expressed struggles based on ability, Robert noted that the cost of less social interaction as a result of pursuing excellence in dance took a heavier toll on him than expected.

> I look around, everyone else in high school can go out to wherever and whenever they want and do fun stuff. All my evenings and weekends are devoted to ballet classes. For me, going out is hardly an option. It is difficult for me because friends around me are happy to be lured to go out to do average "teenager" stuff.

When they were asked to discuss how the general Canadian public views dance, participants' responses varied. Their opinions regarding public views on dance should not be generalized; nonetheless, they can serve as a way to better understand how adolescent males think about the general perception of dance in Canada. Many of them considered Canada as a multicultural country, and therefore Canadians were more likely to accept dance as part of their culture and were willing to see all kinds of dances. However, participants felt that many Canadians had only a superficial understanding of dance. Regardless of their ethnic background, young people did not seem to perceive dance as a legitimate profession. The participants could tell by the way others talked about dance. As one participant noted, expressions like "artsy," "fun," "childish," "cool," or "mesmerizing" showed these opinions. They thought that dance was easy and people on the stage were just having fun. Carter expressed,

> I think that most Canadians don't understand dance ... When they see their kids dancing, they are excited. They don't usually get the meaning or implication of the dance on stage.

Some participants complained that Canadians in general failed to recognize the importance of dance and its role in developing knowledge. That might explain, as one of the participants commented, why no one thought that Canada had made any important contributions to the dance world. David mentioned,

> People from Russia are born to do ballet and [some] dancers in the US are celebrities ... Chinese, Indians, and Greeks are good at keeping their heritage [traditional and ethnic dance]. There are a lot of famous dance stars who are not Canadians. Few dancers were famous in Canada and when they [Canadian dancers] perform in other places, they are usually nobody.

A few students including Robert and Alan responded from a different perspective. They did not consider themselves able to comment on the general Canadian public view of dance because they had only lived in Toronto and were only high school students. They could only say that Toronto had a bigger focus on the arts than other, smaller cities in Canada. Robert assumed that people in the remote areas of Canada might have different views or, even worse, no attitude about dance. He commented that it could be really scary when people have no attitude at all towards dance, not even a bad attitude; they simply don't care.

Jim was a charismatic young male student who had many friends at Rosedale and other schools. In his last year at the school, he became the vice president of Rosedale Students' Union. Born to a large family, he heard more than enough comments about how others saw dance. Jim described,

When I tell people that I dance, they would look at me [as if I were] weird. They would go crazy and wild when I tell them I do hip hop. A totally different story if I let them know that I am doing ballet. There is only good [hip hop] and bad [ballet]. They assume you do one way or the other. If you say that you are doing ballet, they suspect that you can only do ballet and you are strange. On the same token, when you say that you dance hip hop, they would think that you have no dance training but just play with hip hop tricks.

Ballet seemed to be the hardest style for boys to accept.

Dance may be interpreted differently by the public; however, the participants in this research were united when talking about existing stereotypes or biases against males who choose dance as a profession. Although they did not always specify what they meant by dance, it seems that when they spoke about "guys in dance" or "male dancers," they indirectly or directly referred to professional male dancers in ballet and modern. They reported that they commonly heard words such as "egoistic," "self-centred," "homosexual," "weird," and "feminine" when others were speaking about males in dance.

Five participants experienced name-calling personally or heard about it happening to others (see Fig. 6.1). They spoke about the numerous misconceptions and misunderstandings that others had about males in dance. Tom figured that stereotypes came from a twisted American culture, which deemed certain fields as "single gender preferred professions." Carol O'Donnell (1984), in *The Basis of the Bargain: Gender, Schooling, and Jobs*, and Jackie Blount (2000), in "Spinsters, Bachelors, and Other Gender Transgressors in School Employment, 1850–1990," have presented abundant examples and arguments that support Tom's opinion about the concept of gender and profession in American culture. Still, participants were surprised and puzzled to hear that people would call boys in dance "gay" since they danced in a room full of girls. "It doesn't really make any sense," as Tom commented.

Guys in dance are seen as homosexuals or they are just metrosexual. These people don't act as "manly" as other normal folks. I think this stereotype comes from the way dance is looked upon. It is so gentle and delicate ... I think that Americans influence Canadians a lot in terms of stereotyping homosexuality on male dancers.

Anne Flintoff (1991) pointed out in the *British Journal of Physical Education* that there is nothing new or unconventional about people

Fig. 6.1. Perception of stereotypes in dance

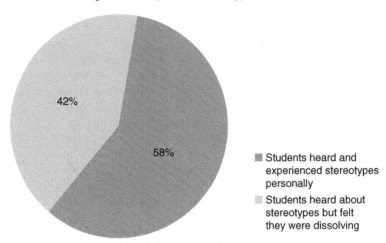

labelling males in dance homosexual, particularly in a North American setting where sports are valued and preferred by the majority of males. That theory has been repeatedly tested and confirmed by other scholars, including Michael Gard (2003b) and Robert Connell (1995). In "Cool Guys, Swots and Wimps: The Interplay of Masculinity and Education," Robert Connell (1989) talked about "equal opportunity and sex-role theories" and he looked at schools as masculinity-making devices – sports are glorified mainly by men. Participating in or watching sports becomes a way for them to defend their masculinity. Dance, on the other hand, is portrayed as an emotional expression, as Joan Ross Acocella (1995) mentioned in her article "Real Men Don't Point Their Feet." Joellen Meglin (1994) presented similar theories in "Gender Issues in Dance Education." Consequently, many males choose not to participate in dance.

Wilson also indicated sexism as a source:

> I feel it is kind of sex stereotyping in dance. I figure that if I were a girl, they would assume that I am doing ballet and it is normal for a girl to do ballet, not a man.

Moving away from gender, Jim suggested that racial identity was a main cause for stereotyping:

I am a guy – a black guy, people will have more chances of guessing that I am doing hip hop or something that is more macho. It seems that my skin culture does not match certain dance forms.

Seven students admitted that they knew about stereotypes in dance. However, they considered them to be gradually dissolving for various reasons. Liam put forward immigration as a factor:

People in general would think that male dancers are more girly. That stereotype is kind of disappearing. I think that immigration does play a role in the changing process. In some European countries, ballet plays a much more important role in the society. Canada gets people from all over the world and it helps break the stereotypes.

Robert speculated that the increasing number of male participants in dance effectively eliminated stereotypical views:

There are many more boys in dance compared to before. Rosedale, for example has more than fifty boys … It's like they are everywhere at this school … With that number, it gets hard for that stereotype to stick.

Kyle suggested political factors:

Kings in old times danced first [see, for instance, Louis XIV]. After they died, other nobles were not allowed to dance. Instead, they told women to dance as a form of entertainment and that is the culture we inherited. I think males can be beautiful and masculine while dancing on the stage. We just need another king, or an important politician in today's sense, to change the tide.

Some participants began to consider it quite special to be a male dance student. Carter, for example, felt great when dancing with many girls. While he admitted his differences compared with female dance students in terms of flexibility and body structure, he pointed out the strength and explosive energy he released while executing certain jumps. "That makes me myself," he asserted.

Several participants expressed that watching many superb male dancers performing a variety of dances (online or on TV) gradually changed their original attitude towards males in dance. David even suggested that males were finally making a comeback in dance:

> For the last four years, the winner of the American popular TV show *So You Think You Can Dance* [has] been all males. We are regaining ground.

However, when that show's cameras scan over the audience of hundreds of spectators, it is not difficult to notice that females dominate the audience. If most viewers and callers who directly affect the results of the dance competition are women, it might explain why men have claimed all the top prizes in recent years. Nonetheless, we have to recognize the increasing popularity of male dancers and the unarguably growing number of males who have an interest in dance.

Despite the stereotypes of males in dance, after several months of training, adolescent male dance students recognized the advantages that they had in dance. Most of them had heard about the shortage of male dancers, and they saw a potential advantage in their career prospects. Seven participants expressed that the shortage of male dancers actually awarded them with better opportunities in this competitive profession. Liam stated,

> I know that there are not as many men in the dance world. Male dancers are a hot commodity. Men are needed to play lead roles, like female[s] can't take all the parts. In some cases, men are required. It is almost like the rareness that it is really good to have males who can really dance in this profession.

Tom also agreed with Liam, describing male dancers as a "rare species" in the profession. He speculated that males would find it much easier to get a call for a ballet or an opera audition. Kyle further added that because of the small number of male dancers, "there are more open windows and doors in terms of getting a job."

Robert not only talked about the advantages of being a male in the profession; he also expressed his excitement and pride in being a male dance student. He became a more confident person when he received compliments from his Opera Atelier dance teacher, who believed in him even though he started his dance training late. This male teacher, who had gone through many auditions, became an inspirational figure for Robert:

> When there is less resource, demand goes up ... I hope that one day I could be able to follow my dance master to go to New York to watch performances and take classes there. My dance teacher at the Opera Atelier tells me "you

may not think that you are in a fully professional program but the fact that you are a male, you will stand out. There might be people around who have not seen you before who would look or assess you when you dance for their choreographies. They may hire you right there." For me, just hearing it makes me excited.

While agreeing that male dancers had an advantage in prospective careers, Carter and Jim considered that a double-edged sword. Since there are often very few males in auditions, they tend to stand out and so it is difficult to hide any mistakes. In fact, it could leave them vulnerable to a certain extent. Carter said,

Yes, you will get a lot of special treatment … You are being noticed more because there are not many of us [male dancers] on stage. It is a double-edged sword to me because you can be really good and standing out while dancing with many girls and it could be really awful when you make mistakes. We are just more noticeable, I think. It is more challenging to be male dancers because it requires us to do much more than girls.

Four students thought of male dancers as having better physical strength. Some males, being bigger and stronger, could jump higher and lift other dancers with less difficulty. One participant, Wilson, suggested that just being a dance student made him look stronger when compared with males who did not take dance. As a result, he found himself more popular among girls. Michael, on the other hand, looked at the advantage from the point of view of the male body:

Men are more biologically designed to do dance. For example, ballet is a lot about upper body strengthened dance form and boys are really good at that. Men are also good at lifting and supporting others in modern and jazz.

At this point, it is evident that these boys were becoming activists in promoting the participation of males in dance. For most, this change in attitude came after participating in dance classes, rehearsals, and performances. It takes time, though, as many of these students expressed that their initial dance experiences were usually less than desirable.

These dance students were almost in total agreement when asked what advice they would give to the majority of male students who had never taken dance. Their message was clear: "try it out yourself." All of them recommended that other males take dance and try it before making a judgment based on what they thought, which might not be accurate.

Some participants wanted others to know that taking dance was one of the best choices they had ever made. They became more encouraged when they saw many other boys in dance at the school. Furthermore, participants admitted that taking dance made them more popular among girls. Wilson suggested,

> You should try it because it is really a fun experience to have. It helps you control your body more. Oh, yeah, girls like guys who can dance ... It [dance] makes me popular.

Junior students who had the least dance experience would often compare dance to gym. To many, a general physical education course had been their only choice since kindergarten. In comparison, they credited dance with strengthening more and different muscles than gym would have. These young men admitted that dance forced them to think more intensely when moving, something they had never done before. As a result, they became more aware of the way they walked down the street or how they were standing at a bus stop. Alan said, "I have to constantly think about my alignment, posture, steps, and much more. While in gym, I feel like a machine repeating things over and over again."

The students suggested that more boys in dance would effectively reduce stereotypes against male dancers. One junior student even recommended a male dance school with a focus on male dance curriculum. He argued that if that happened, everything would be fundamentally changed. "People walking into a male dance class would probably not let out comments such as 'look at that weirdo.' Instead, people would look at me as a dancer with lots of spectacular muscles as the evidence of rigorous dance training." In fact, all-male dance classes at the pre-professional level do exist at institutions outside of public schools, and these classes are especially beneficial in training males to pursue dance professionally. With the help of social media (such as Facebook and Twitter) and other technology, one can easily locate all-male dance classes, which are common in China, Cuba, Russia, and some east European countries. Speaking of media and technology, all students in this study unanimously agreed that new media greatly affected people's views of male dancers, especially in recent years. For many students, the Internet became the only place for them to watch videos of and share ideas about dance. "There were many celebrated choreographies online for people to see," one of the students claimed. The use of technology in dance classes helped them to be more engaged. Their thinking reveals the great value they placed on technology in general and provides some insights into how to better engage adolescent males in dance. To a certain extent, the students believed that such technology could be one of the means of breaking down social barriers towards males in dance, as it did in some ways for them.

Among the 12 participants, four different views emerged about the impact of media and technology on male dancers. Three views – that media helped to expand viewership of, normalize, and promote male dancers – were on the positive side; the last one, creation of more bias, represented a different point of view (see Fig. 6.2).

Media and technology has expanded the viewership of males in dance. It has challenged the traditional perspective that people used to have about male dancers. Media has also opened new windows and doors for cross-cultural and regional experiences. Jim mentioned seeing a YouTube video clip about a dance troupe based in Denmark. He also talked about the increasing popularity of the hit show *So You Think You Can Dance*:

> I was shocked to see the way these guys [were] dancing. Their movements were strong and precise that they looked like robots. It was amazing. If it were not for the Internet, I would not be able to know that. Internet greatly affected my way of seeing male dancers in Denmark. Shows like *So You Think You Can Dance* get millions of hits outside its birth place, the United States. People from Australia, New Zealand, and China click their mouse to find out who is the best dancer.

Participants also spoke about a group of black male dancers called Signature who performed on the British hit show *Britain's Got Talent*. They admitted that if it were not for YouTube, fewer people would be exposed to such groups because the show was based in London, England. Such media also expands the audience for professional performances. Participants argued that the cost of tickets made it increasingly difficult to be able to enjoy live theatre. Although technology can never replace the experience of viewing a live performance, cyber viewing is affordable and accessible for most people in North America, whether in school or at home, and so nearly anyone can watch the best male dancers performing right in front of their eyes. Carter stated,

Fig. 6.2. Media and technology's impact on male dance students

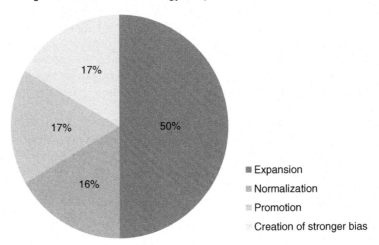

Most families have at least a computer or a TV at home and they can watch these shows. I believe that many people have "one-on-one" dance experience because of the wide spread of technology. It changes people's view on male dancers. People would see male dancers as more of human beings rather than just a "stuck-up" [arrogant or snobbish] people on stage.

Two senior dance students, Robert and Liam, discussed how media and technology have effectively normalized male dancers as ordinary folks in public and on stage. They both thought that technology does a superb job of promoting male dancers in remote areas where people might not have access to regular venues, such as large dance theatres. Through media and technology, viewers can learn about different styles of dance and different types of male dancers; some are more muscular than others, and while some might look more feminine, not all male dancers do. Liam further stated,

These shows have a huge impact on how people see males in dance. For example, *So You Think You Can Dance* features many different kinds of male dancers. Audiences get to know them as normal people. I think that the vast majority of male dancers on *So You Think You Can Dance* are not in any way to be described as feminine or gay. The show breaks down the stereotypes right there.

The majority of the students considered such media and technology to be major contributors in promoting a better image of male dancers in our society. Participants communicated that the show *So You Think You Can Dance* features many great male dancers on the stage, which in part challenges people's old thinking that men are not capable of dancing. Gradually more and more people seem to have accepted the fact, promoted by media, that males can dance and some of them can do just as well as females, if not better. The spread of technology has effectively reduced biases that once existed in our society. Alan said,

> These media shows definitely help get the message out that males can dance. Without media publicity, I don't think we would have gone this far in terms of our perceptions on male dancers ... Usually, when we talk about male dancers, people would only remember those superstars such as Gene Kelly and Mikhail Baryshnikov. Now, they would be more tempted to accept the fact that other regular males [like me] can dance, too.

Wilson talked about watching a video clip titled "Evolution of Dance" by Judson Laipply on YouTube a couple of years ago. Almost 295 million people viewed that short clip in its first eight years – more than eight times the current population of all of Canada. Wilson described the video:

> It shows a guy doing dances from the 50s to the present. Millions and millions [of] people [have] watch[ed] this dance over the Internet. It is really funny especially he is a regular white bald man in his forties. Someone that you don't think can dance. It really makes me want to move at the same time.

In 2012, just six months after it was released on YouTube, "Gangnam Style," which featured the "horse dance" and rapping by Korean pop star Psy, became the most-viewed video online – with over one billion visits.

It was intriguing to discover that two male dance students saw the unjust side of the media's impact on male dancers. They indicated that media has actually created more biases against males in dance. Michael pointed out that media "flipped around" the images and stereotypes of male dancers in order to make them look more controversial to boost their viewing rate. David further noted that most of the people who watched the show *So You Think You Can Dance* were already in dance (although that is debatable) and that they had biased opinions towards female dancers as being better than males. David said,

Some dancers [males and females] claim that "if I don't dance, I will die." I don't think so. If I don't dance, I will still do music or acting. They purposely choose men saying that to make them more emotional, girly, and naive.

Kyle did not take dance in grade 9, but he was fascinated by other males performing on stage at Rosedale Heights. He decided to take dance in grade 10. He commented that it is never too late to start:

I think it is definitely a great thing to start to take dance. I see many other males starting to take dance at Rosedale and they are looking good on stage. It really inspired me on that note. I recommend [to] other boys that [you should] never think that you are too late to dance. You can start even at my level, which is grade 10. Every male can be looking good in dance, of course if he works hard.

Identifying dance as an adventure in his life, Liam had these words for others:

It is fun. You don't have to be serious about dance to enjoy it. It is a great experience … If there is something else that you are interested [in], go do that. If not, I recommend you to give dance a try.

His message was similar to what Michael recommended to other males who might be interested in taking dance:

Take it for a year and try it. If you love it, go for it. Just go for it! If you don't like it, well, that is how you think. I took [dance] for a year as a tryout. I fell in love with dance. That's how I got into dance. Just give it a try. There is nothing bad [that] will happen, I guarantee. It got me into shape and made me a better human being.

Senior students cautioned potential male dance students not to be fooled by stereotypes. Their messages seemed to carry a word of warning as they knew how much work was needed in order to get better in dance, often including extra classes within and outside of school. Nonetheless, they suggested others give it a try. They argued that if boys did not try, they would never know if they liked it. If they tried and did not like it, they could always do something else. As late starters in dance, they admitted that taking dance was the most rewarding yet challenging decision they had ever made. "You got to work really hard if you are serious about it," Jim confessed. As a senior dance student, Carter delivered a similar message:

I would definitely encourage them [other adolescent males] to try it [dance]. It is challenging and a lot more work than you expected. At the same time, it is extremely rewarding. Don't base on the stereotype or your opinion you had before toward male dancers. You can never experience that exhilarating feeling until you give it a try. There are tons of classes around and you should give it a shot.

Robert, who wanted to become a professional ballet dancer, recommended other boys not start with ballet. As a young boy, he did not set his heart on ballet. He was into breakdancing before falling in love with ballet much later. He compared his spending time and money for ballet classes to others shopping for boots, both of which result in acquiring something for the body. However, taking ballet to him was more than a possession or getting something he could hold on to; it provided a much more fulfilling or enlightening experience, which helped him to better understand others and himself. "It is a balance between body and mind." Admitting that ballet might not be attractive to beginner boys, he advised other choices in dance:

Try it. It does not have to be ballet to start. Try something masculine like hip hop or popping, which are not feminine look[ing] at all. There is so much to do in dance and it is almost foolish not to try but to assume. It [dance] will definitely make you as a better person in general. It is worth it, I believe in it.

7
Dance Experience and Dance Class

Dancing with others along with music is quite different from pulsating alone with earplugs in. The sweat, loud music, heartbeats, instructor's comments, peers' gazing, and humidity in the room actually create a magnetic environment. Being in a dance class is a unique experience that is beyond words. According to many boys in this study, their initial dance experiences, which occurred at different times, in various locations and settings, were critical to how they perceived dance later on. The majority of the students indicated that their first dance experience occurred in public school. Among them, four boys attended a dance workshop during elementary school as an after-school activity, and three began dancing in high school. Of the four students who experienced dance in elementary school, three expressed fairly positive comments. They also indicated that their dance experience in elementary school was mostly short and inconsistent but had memorable moments. Alan recalled,

> My first dance experience was when I was in elementary school [extracurricular]. Two teachers, one used to be a dancer, rented a dance studio outside. There were 35 of us cramped into a small room. It was pretty basic that we just followed steps to a song. I could not even describe the style of the dance. The school wanted to give us a taste of real dance class. I enjoyed it quite a bit even though it was short.

David had his first dance experience in grade 3 when a volunteer came to his class and taught dance workshops after school. That dancer did it just for the love of teaching. David was especially interested in the "moonwalk":

I was quite impressed with his "moonwalk." Honestly, my class did not like it that much but I enjoyed it quite a bit. I really liked the moonwalk look and I thought it was really cool ... The first time I danced was a scary experience. I had absolutely no idea what to expect. I thought that I was going to walk into a room filled with amazing experienced dancers and that a dance teacher would expect so much from me. I thought that my girl classmates would be much better than boys. It was not the case at all. I ended up to be one of the best. At least I got the moonwalk move faster than everyone else in the class!

The only one to recall a negative experience in elementary school, Liam, claimed that he never thought about dance until one of his bossy friends dragged him to a dance class when he was a grade 5 student.

George and Carter both had their first dance experience at Rosedale, although they arrived at the experience through different paths. George took gymnastics and drama when he was young but never tried dance. He mentioned that he used to watch the Cirque du Soleil shows on CBC every Saturday night with his parents. He started to take dance at Rosedale in grade 9 but counted those Saturday nights as his first acquaintance with dance, although he did not do it physically.

Carter, whose first dance experience was in the grade 10 dance open course at Rosedale, never thought that he would take dance so seriously. He originally came to Rosedale to study drama because he dreamed of becoming a movie star one day. His mother, a former professional ballerina, was surprised to hear that Carter took up the challenge to do the grade 11 dance major after just one year of training. He described his first dance experience as not easy:

> I remember that I did every possible thing wrong. Everyone was moving one way and I was moving the other. It [dance] was really hard. I did not know why but somehow I fell in love with dancing. I still vividly remember that chassé was really hard. I practiced that traveling movement over and over again in my room until late night. I wanted to get it done perfectly. To me, it was really difficult.

Michael had a painful and unforgettable experience when he took dance for the first time. Never having danced in his life, he thought the class would be really easy and that a dance credit in high school could be a "free ride." His lack of respect towards dance changed as he quickly realized how "muscular" dance actually was.

I had no idea what to expect and I did not think dance was hard. It was a Friday afternoon during the first week of my high school. Teachers were cruising through outlines and course expectations. I thought dance was the same. It was not at all. The warm up alone was so intense and after class, I felt like jelly. My whole body was in so much pain. Thank God it was a Friday because I could not even walk for the next two days. I spent most of the time recovering on the bed that weekend. When I went to the washroom, I had to walk really slowly because all my muscles are in pain. It was so bad that I could not even make a bowel movement ... My parents laughed at me and commented that it was long overdue.

Five participants said that their first dance experience was family related. Some danced during family vacations or gatherings while others participated in dance camps or creative movement workshops. Robert and Tom shared similar stories. Their parents took them to see dance performances (such as *Stomp*, *Tap Dog*, and *Nutcracker*) and both got interested in dance. They each took a couple of dance classes after watching the performances but quit shortly after. Robert confessed that dancing with many girls made him feel bored and that he had a hard time legitimizing continuing to dance. His feeling of being marginalized because he was involved in an activity participated in mostly by females is reflected in Christine Williams's (1995) book, *Still a Man's World: Men Who Do Women's Work*. Williams looked at males in female-dominated professions – librarians, elementary school teachers, nurses, and social workers – and used the term "masculinity in 'feminine' occupations" to address occupational segregation and gender inequality issues. Some scholars argue that the early focus on creative dance is one of the reasons boys quit dancing, because of a lack of structure at that initial stage, but in Robert's case, he still chose to quit dance after doing much more than creative dance. From what Robert shared, he might have struggled with his own identity and self-worth in dance, a theory argued by Michael Gard (2001, 2003a), or he might have felt alone and insecure because he was the only boy in the class.

Wilson and Alan, on the other hand, had their first dance experience while their families were on vacation. This tends to be a classic story shared by many children around the world. Wilson said,

My first dance experience took place when I was a little boy on a travel trip with my parents to Jamaica. I was about six years old. There was a little dance club in town that me and my family went there together after dinner. It was really fun and that was my first time dancing in a club. I had some pictures on that but I could not remember what types of dance I did. Maybe I was just moving my body crazily.

Jim had a different first dance experience from everyone else in the group. Instead of watching dance on TV or on stage, or being inspired by a skilful dancer, he was put into dance by his parents as a form of therapy to help control his temper at only five years old.

> I used to fight a lot and was best described as an angry boy. My parents put me into a dance program to see if I could channel my anger to some other things to better use my anger. My first dance experience had nothing to do with any specific form of technique. Someone simply turned on the music and we just danced to it ... With a lot of freedom, it worked as I danced my hardest to burn out most of my angry feelings. In the end, I was happy. I considered that was my first dance experience.

Jim's parents not only saw dance as expression, they also went a step further and looked at dance as a form of therapeutic treatment for their son to better manage his feelings.

Among the 12 adolescent males who participated in the study, ten decided to take dance at Rosedale the following year, while two decided not to. Of those who chose to dance again, nine were in grade 9 or 10 and would be taking dance again at the grade 10 or 11 level in the 2009–10 school year. The tenth was in his graduating year and taking additional dance classes at the National Ballet School of Canada in the evenings (see Fig. 7.1). This grade 12 student chose to stay behind for a fifth year at Rosedale for extra dance training. He later auditioned for the professional dance training program at the National Ballet School of Canada. He attended that daytime program for one year and took evening classes at Opera Atelier before being spotted by Marshall Pynkoski, the artistic director of Opera Atelier. After training with Opera Atelier at various levels – as a co-op student, in full-time dance classes, and as an apprentice – he became a dancer in Pynkoski's ballet company.

Of the other nine students who continued at Rosedale, six signed up for the all-boys dance class for grades 9 and 10 students and three opted for mixed-gender dance classes at the grade 11 level. Reasons for them to continue dancing were quite similar, with personal enjoyment (mental benefits) and positive change to their body (physical benefits) being the two main ones.

Six boys were impressed by how much they had accomplished in dance physically in such a short time (from one to two years). They felt that

Fig. 7.1. Students' future dance plans

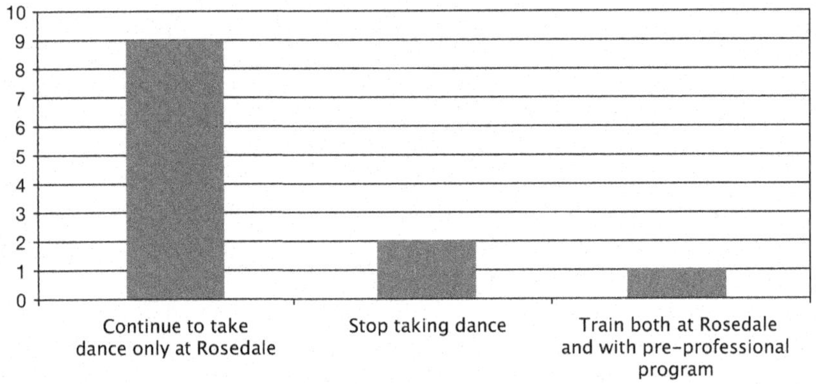

taking dance was a fulfilling and tangible experience in which they could see progress and improvement on a daily basis. Alan mentioned,

> When I first took dance, I was a one-step and two-step person … Just in one year, I certainly see me growing as a dancer. I have to maintain the same level of training, flexibility, coordination, and strength.

Jim also enjoyed the excitement of the physical aspect. He added,

> I'd do it again because I found it was a good workout. I enjoy meeting physical challenges in dance as well as learning new steps and moves … I am amazed to find out that after a short while, I don't have to pay attention to my body parts as they kind of channel themselves automatically and smoothly … As time goes on, my awkward feeling slowly disappears.

Michael's comments were similar to several others in the all-boys dance class who had a positive experience, but he could not elaborate on his feelings as eloquently. He had a hard time explaining his rationale for continuing to take dance in high school.

> Honestly, I did not know why I took dance again in grade 10. I was really bad at it first but, there was something … It was like being reborn when I did it

... It made me feel so good. I did not know how to describe it. I just saw dance was not something I would give up.

Many boys expressed that while taking dance, they became more confident and capable human beings. Two boys who chose to continue taking dance were influenced by their friends. Both were surrounded by friends who were actively involved in dance and were encouraged to take dance again because their friends saw they had potential. Diana Kendall (2005) suggested in her book *Sociology in Our Times* that dance is an important component in the lives of adolescent males; it becomes a way for them to build trust among each other. Liam recalls,

> A senior student in Rosedale who was in grade 11 at the time and going into grade 12 dance major came to me and said, "I really want you to be in one of my choreographic workshop dance pieces because I like the way you dance and express yourself." He was a friend of my older brother since they went through the same middle school together. He came to my dance concert and saw me dancing and complimented me on that. Just the thought that I would actually be needed to do something at the school played [a] big part in my decision to continue to dance this year.

Although Liam eventually recognized himself as a potential dancer or was seen as one by his friends, his initial decision to come to Rosedale was a different story. As a grade 8 student, he did not see himself as a dancer at all. He had two options: attending a school with all his old friends or going to Rosedale. He picked the second choice and became the only student from his old school to attend an arts-focused high school. His choice might have been due to the compliments from his brother's friend, who saw Liam's performance at a local dance studio when Liam was in grade 8, and could also have been influenced by his mother, who had been championing his involvement in dance and the arts. Either way, he found himself in dance and continuing in dance.

The two students, both going into grade 11, who decided not to take dance the following year claimed that limited course selection was to blame. Both stated that if they were to take dance again, they wanted to be in an all-boys dance class. However, the all-boys dance classes were offered only at the grade 9 and 10 level and they did not want to take it as a non-credited course.

According to a guidance counsellor, if students were to take the all-boys dance class again after grade 10, they would not get any high school credit.[1] This certainly turned students away; in the past, quite a few students had expressed their desire to take the all-boys dance class but could not do it because it was deemed as non-credit. It may be beneficial for administrators at the school to consider opening an all-boys dance class with a senior grade credit, which would encourage more senior boys to continue dancing and would make the whole course selection process more equitable and accessible.

Interviews revealed two different attitudes that emerged as the boys continued to take dance. The older the students were (grade 11 and up), the more eager they were to learn. In contrast, most junior students (grade 9 and 10) had a cause-and-effect attitude, focusing on the positive changes on their physicality and capability in dance.

Senior students expressed that dance was much more challenging when they took it again at the grade 11 and 12 level. Three students were in the dance major class and they had to take ballet, jazz, and modern on a daily basis, as compared to the dance minor track, which required taking dance only two or three times a week. They confessed that their original fun experience was quickly replaced by sweat, hard work, and high expectations to get better and stronger as dance students. Nonetheless, nobody gave up and all were determined to work hard and enjoy the journey. Robert said,

> I really feel that I am part of it [dance] now. The first three years at Rosedale, I felt that I had been trying to dance. I constantly felt that I needed more technique, training, time to practice, etc.; it wasn't until last year or even this year (fifth year at Rosedale) that I start[ed] to feel that I am actually dancing, which is really miraculous. It is indescribable.

Liam also noticed that the more he learned dance, the more he felt he needed to work on becoming a stronger dancer. Dancing at Rosedale for two years made him eager to study harder – not only the technical skills but also the theory behind dance. He constantly looked for opportunities to attend dance classes and workshops in and outside of school. In the summer of 2008, he signed up for an intensive summer school program at Opera Atelier Ballet School to advance his skill and knowledge in ballet. Liam stated,

---

1 Boys at Rosedale can take the junior-level, all-boys dance class more than once but they receive no credit, or a so-called waste-credit, for subsequent classes because they are not needed for high school graduation.

At the Opera Atelier, I learned a huge part of dance all of a sudden ... After attending the intensive dance training, I understood why ballet was the root of every form of dance. There, I did ballet 3 hours a day and 5 times a week, which was really intense. It completely strengthened my technique and helped my whole understanding in dance ... I felt myself more and more into dance. It was incredible and I felt that I was myself whenever I danced.

Junior students (those taking dance less than two years) tended to concentrate on the positive changes that dance had effected in their bodies or on their ability to move or think. All of them were more than satisfied to see the encouraging development of body structures, usually stronger muscles – abdominal, pectorals, quadriceps, and lower legs. Some, like Michael, were glad to see themselves grow as a more confident person:

I was extremely self-conscious when I first took dance in grade 9. I was so concerned about how others looked at me. I hid at the back almost all the time. Now, I am different. I am up at the front [first line] in dance class. I know that this is me and I am in charge. I don't know how but I am glad that things turned out to be like that.

Jim shared a similar comment: "Since I have started it [dance], I am much more confident and I am not scared of dancing in front of an audience anymore."

Both Tom and David thought dance would be an easy school credit. They described the evolution of their dance experience as a new but exciting discovery during their high school years. Initially, they were not serious about dance at all. After a few classes, they both admitted that dance was not effortless as they thought it would be. Their embodied dance experience, involving both physical and mental aspects, altered their attitude about seeing themselves and other males in dance. Dance was no longer an "abnormal" activity but something they would like to explore more. David added,

I never watched dance shows before but I have started to watch contemporary dance on TV ever since I took dance. I even began to take ballet, which was something I would never do in my life if I did not take dance at Rosedale.

Different locations present different challenges, yet almost all boys had positive experiences, notably those in all-boys dance classes. When male students were asked to describe their dance classes in high school, a few expressed minor concerns not regarding dance but about the facility where they danced. The amount of time they spent in dance drastically influenced these boys' engagement from dancing for physical benefit to dancing for the sake of dancing. Students who took the all-boys class in the dance studio expressed noticeably more positive views on dance; "warm," "a sense of community," "brotherhood," "fun," and "joyful" were frequent words they used to talk about the class.

> *Alan:* Everyone seems to be really warm and interested in dancing. Nobody is there for only the credit. It's joyful and it is great for fitness. There is definitely no negativity whatsoever [Illus. 7.1].
>
> *Tom:* I like our class because it is not judgmental in any way. You are free to do whatever you want as long as you try and have a good attitude towards what you are doing [Illus. 7.2].

Jim described the class as a family with a sense of inclusiveness:

> Everyone laughs at each other [in a good way], works together, plays together and of course, dances together. There is no hard feeling or tension but a giant group of males doing what they want to do. It makes me feel good, actually great. I see this class as a place I can go to and leave all my problems at the door and enjoy myself completely in dance.

A few boys in this class expressed that they focused so much on dance steps that they could not notice anything else happening in the class. George and David admitted that they could barely process the detailed instructions given during the dance class. They both found it unique because they usually could not focus that long in regular classrooms (e.g., French, math, English).

Three out of 12 participants – one each in grade 10, grade 11, and grade 12 – took dance in mixed-gender classes. Liam, who was in a grade 10 dance major mixed-gender class, had the least dance training compared to his senior dance friends at the school. He talked about his initial challenge in taking dance at Rosedale:

> When I first came to this dance major class, the biggest deal was being the only guy. Many people told me that you are in a class full of girls and that must be great. Actually, it's not. It's embarrassing most of the time. Being the only boy makes me feel really ... really small. Being the only guy kind of

Illus. 7.1. Boys practise split jumps in a ballet class

Illus. 7.2. All-boys dance class students practise their movements
in the dance studio

make[s] others and I think "Am I weird because I take dance, which is so different from other guys?" I wonder if I tell others that I take dance, would they think that I am a gay.

In this case, Liam quickly gained his confidence in dance. He added,

[As] I grow older and I get more mature, I start to realize that it really does not matter about how others think about me but how I enjoy what I love to do. I slowly get over that discomfort feeling by going to dance class more often and meeting other male dancers and teachers who are confident about what they do. I start to realize that it does not really matter if you are the only guy in the class. I have to convince myself that I am no different than others. I begin to see that being a male in the dance major class is a privilege.

Both Carter, grade 11, and Robert, grade 12, stated that they were quite comfortable when dancing with girls in dance major classes, each of which has approximately 25 female dance students and 1 male. They also attended extra dance classes outside Rosedale. Robert started his intense ballet training at Opera Atelier, with which he performed periodically as an apprentice while finishing high school. Carter began his

African and modern dance training with Collective of Black Artists (COBA).[2] They shared similar views on dance.

Carter: I am so focused that I don't really pay too much attention when I take dance. Partially it is [in]tense and I have to concentrate to get the movement right.

  Robert: I would say that the ballet classes need a lot more intense focus. At the same time, I feel so relaxed that I forget about anything else. It becomes only ballet at that moment and I am part of it.

There are three types of dance classes offered to boys in the school: mixed-gender dance class (usually at grade 11 and 12 level) and two separate all-boys dance classes, one of which takes place in a regular dance studio and the other in the gym (Illus. 7.3). Adolescent male dance students took pleasure in dancing with peers and watching one another's progress regardless of which class they were in. They particularly enjoyed the feeling of their body temperature changing from cold to warm as the class proceeded to more active and larger movements. It was particularly obvious in the winter as many boys complained of being tired or sleepy at the beginning of the dance class but got sweaty and energized by the end. Having a live accompanist – a pianist in ballet and a drummer in modern dance – made them feel more energized and engaged.

A few students in the all-boys classes that took place in the big dance studio complained about the smell of the room. Those who danced in the gym did not talk about the smell but grumbled about the condition of the floor. More than 800 students used that gym every day for their physical education courses. In modern dance class, students had to dance in bare feet on the same floor used by students who wore all types of shoes while playing floor hockey or other games. By the end of the class, dance students' feet were either hurt (usually by wood chips) or stained black by the dirty floor.

Wilson, Kyle, and Michael were among 20 adolescent males taking an all-boys dance class in the gym when the study took place. With an increasing number of students signing up for dance, the school ran out of

---

2 Collective of Black Artists (COBA) is a Toronto-based dance company. It was founded in 1993 by four black dancers to build a platform for dance creations that reflect their values, heritage, and culture.

Illus. 7.3. Males in dance classes (mixed-gender and all-boys)

studio space for the growing classes. In early September 2008, the school administrators designated the gym as an alternative space for the second all-boys class. Unlike regular dance studios, the gym in many ways created an unpleasant environment for a dance class. For example, it was equipped not with a sprung floor[3] but with a regular hardwood floor with numerous splinters and gum leftovers. There were no windows and no sound system. In the ballet unit, students had to use hockey nets as barres for balancing. Numerous times, classes were cut short because of sports games.

Nonetheless, participants in this group still presented positive comments when they described their dance class. Other than discussing what they experienced in dance, participants focused on their physical and mental transformations through taking dance. Wilson described dancing in the gym as like pursuing freedom. "It was not easy. It hurts and it even burns my skin when I first started," he recalled. The gym was the coldest place in the school because of its size and barrenness, with only a basketball hoop on each side. In the modern dance unit, students had to take off their shoes and socks and dance on the freezing floor. Although the dance teacher made some adjustments, such as encouraging students to wear socks at the beginning of the class, these could not prevent students from getting splinters. Students were still happy as class unfolded. Michael noted,

> At the start of the class, I felt cold, lazy, and slightly depressed. I did not even want to move. During the class, I began to sweat and I started to feel pumped. By the end of the class, I was the happiest person on earth! The music was loud and I really enjoyed it. It could smell bad when some guys in the class did not wear deodorant. Yet, it was relatively ok compared to last year [when he took an all-boys dance class in a large dance studio] because we danced in a gigantic gym.

While they enjoyed dancing together, many boys spoke about the all-boys dance class being "overly muscular" in terms of its smell. It was not an issue in the gym because of its gigantic space. However, it was suffocating in a dance studio soon after warm-up. As Jim noted, the studio quickly became unbearable even for the most tolerant person.

---

3 A sprung floor is a floor that absorbs shocks and it provides a softer feel for dancers. Sprung floors enhance dance performance and reduce injuries and accidents.

One of the boys mentioned that male students in the all-boys classes tended not to use deodorant. In fact, many of them had no knowledge of what it was. No matter how repeatedly the teacher encouraged them to use deodorant, only a few cooperated. In contrast, the male students in mixed-gender dance classes quickly learned the "trick" to make themselves smell good (using deodorant) without the teacher saying a word.

Six participants expressed that they faced challenges ranging from the intellectual approach to dance, such as choreography, to the type of dance, such as ballet. Ballet was a major issue, with almost every boy complaining about it. They initially thought ballet was easy but their impressions quickly crumbled when they executed their first plié. Both Carter and Tom talked about the complexity and precision that ballet technique class required. Carter said,

> Getting in details and I am not a detail-oriented person. Ballet is hard as there are so many little precise things that I have to remember when dancing. For example, you have to think 10 things at once even when you make a simple ballet pose [back straight, posture, turnout, alignment, etc.].

Liam and Alan thought learning choreography was the most challenging part in dance. They both found it hard to be correct in alignment and posture while standing on the dance floor. Applying all the details and instructions was even harder. Remembering movements and steps in choreography while attempting to address all the requirements was the hardest. Furthermore, switching from one style to the other, jazz to ballet for instance, was like relearning everything altogether. Liam explained,

> Choreography, I thought I had it because I know that I can learn/pick up and memorize movements pretty quickly. However, from jazz going into another genre is a totally different experience. Although it looks like the same, it is not. To me, it is relearning everything, from step to step and move to move [Illus. 7.4].

Flexibility seemed to be an unreachable goal for some of the participants. Interestingly, some participants at the beginning used gender to excuse their lack of flexibility. They would argue that boys were naturally less flexible than girls and hence they should not bother stretching. Nevertheless, as time went by, they realized how important flexibility was to the progression of their dance skills. Their more mature thinking can be partially credited to a field trip to the National Ballet of Canada,

Illus. 7.4. Male dancers practise krumping for the year-end performance

where they saw professional male dancers warm up and dance. Watching dance clips on the Internet and on TV, as well as reading dance materials, also helped them understand that they could gain flexibility by working hard.

> *Jim:* Ouch, flexibility! I could do the movement, follow the steps, dance somewhat smoothly, and feel the music but I am not flexible. I wish I were more flexible so that I could actually dance better than I am doing right now.

George used his grandmother as an inspirational figure:

> My grandmother is 86 years old and she still dances. She does stretch the way that many younger ones would not believe ... She can definitely do more things than I do. Being alone for a number of years [since her husband passed away], she has not had any problems [physically]. She does line dancing and tap.

Clearly, the male dance students participating in this study came from different backgrounds and experienced dance classes at Rosedale Heights in various ways. A few boys had no dance experience before high school. Most boys had positive initial dance experiences while only one had a negative experience. However, they all came to enjoy dance in high school. Hence, there seems to be no correlation between boys' first dance experience or lack thereof and their desire to dance in high school. It should be noted that when looking at the boys with no prior dance experience, one in particular had a relatively more stressful entrance into dance at high school. Looking at their backgrounds, it seems that students who have no family ties to dance may have more psychological struggles with the idea of being in dance. Boys who come with previous dance experience, even just a little, show a much smoother transition, and as a result, they enjoy taking dance earlier and enter the "flow" stage sooner. There was a difference between gender-specific and mixed-gender dance classes; boys in mixed-gender classes were at the outset hugely influenced by the gender imbalance and needed to shift their thinking in order to continue to dance. The sense of community in the all-boys dance class offered a degree of security, which allowed those boys to enter into a "flow" where they wholeheartedly focused on their steps. This attitude towards dance, where embodied enjoyment was the primary benefit, came more easily for some students, particularly in senior years. Others, particularly junior dance students, initially appreciated the straightforward physical results of dance, such as muscle development, and a sense of community, especially in all-boys dance classes. Meanwhile, it became apparent that venue, whether conducive to dance or not, did not affect the boys' positive experiences with dance. Other points of interest were the boys' feelings towards choreography and flexibility. Educators need to be mindful of how male and female dancers differ in these areas and to observe closely and reassess frequently to ensure that their choreography and flexibility expectations provide the appropriate amount of challenge.

8
Show Time

All of the participants agreed that performing on stage had a positive impact on their life. The whole process of rehearsing, putting on make-up, costuming, spacing, and warming up for the show was a memorable journey. For many, this was their first time ever dancing on stage in front of others (including family members). Students in grades 9 and 10 admitted that they were surprised to see how much work was required prior to a dance performance (see Illus. 8.1 and 8.2). Kyle noted,

> Year-end dance performance is definitely a highlight of this course. It is really great to get together with all your friends not to fool around like we do at other times. We actually dance on stage. I also like the process of rehearsing for months into the three nights' performances in the end. It teaches me how to be a patient person. I enjoy the backstage warm up and supportive environment around. It's great to get pumped with many others before we get onto the stage.

Wilson shared his contentment when performing on the stage:

> It is so much joy to see everything coming together. It is great to work with the music and media to make our dance look good. I enjoy the end result but not necessarily the rehearsal part. It was boring and gruelling at times. I am glad that I survived, though.

Three months before the year-end performance, all dance students participated in a choreographic workshop show.[1] Wilson compared the

---

1 The choreographic workshop is an annual event at Rosedale that takes place in February. Grade 12 dance major students coordinate the entire show, including auditions, choreography, rehearsals, costumes, lighting, and promotion.

Illus. 8.1. All-boys dance class students practise their year-end dance
performance in the dance studio

two performance experiences, describing the choreographic workshop
show as more nerve-wracking:

> I find it [the choreographic workshop] more stressful because I have to
> dance with others who have years of dance training. I like the year-end
> dance performance because I am dancing with my friends [all boys] who
> share the similar dance level [beginner] as I am at.

When asked about whether the three months of "gruelling" rehearsals
were worthwhile for a two-minute dance piece on stage, many male
dance students said yes. They expressed that the whole journey really
shaped the way they thought about dance. Of course, rehearsals helped
them look better and feel much more confident while performing on
stage (Illus. 8.3).

> *Jim:* The more you look forward to the product, the greater [the] end result
> is going to be. I do value the rehearsal periods as I know that the more we
> practise, the better it gets. We end up to be more satisfied as a result. I know
> it is a fact but I forget at times.

Illus. 8.2. All-boys dance class students practise their year-end dance
performance in the school gym

Male senior dance students (grades 11 and 12) admitted struggles during the choreographic and rehearsal process, but they reached a sense of exhilaration and accomplishment in the end. The whole journey was tough and involved challenges beyond dance, such as teamwork, communication, creativity, and abstract and literal thinking, just to name a few. Carter shared his choreographic journey from an assignment in which students had to design a performance based on a painting.

My group chooses this neo-impressionist art that looks like a tree from far away. When you get closer, it becomes clear that this tree is actually made of different women. It is really cool to reinterpret that through a dance but it was not easy to do with [a] moving body.

Robert recalled one of his grade 11 dance assignments in which he had to create a ballet solo on his own. He found that the experience greatly challenged the way he thought about choreography. During the whole process, he had to constantly readjust his approach to music and to move his body in a way that he was not accustomed to in order to test possibilities. He claimed that the assignment forced him to reconsider dance as the only career that he could do in the future:

Illus. 8.3. All-boys dance class students perform on the stage

Illus. 8.4. Students from both of the all-boys dance classes
make a "snake pose" during the rehearsal

It was a neat experience! I was surprised that I could possibly do that. That experience actually opened the possibilities for me to be a choreographer in the future. I created Mario dance. I listened to the music many times and tried to make it as showy, fun, and goofy as possible. It was a hit in the end and everybody loves the dance.

Interviews with adolescent male dance students showed three distinctive categories of how they felt and thought while dancing on stage. Novice students who were dancing on stage for the first time fell into the freshmen category. Students with two years of dance training or less were identified as connecting individuals. Students with more than two years of dance experience were labelled as self-actualized performers.

Novice students constantly used words such as "nervous," "embarrassing," "exciting," and "fun" to describe their first-time dance experience on stage. These students usually went through three stages – nervousness, excitement, and contentment. For them, performing on stage seemed at first to be an unbearable and unattainable task. Many were really concerned about how they would look and what others would think about their performance. A few minutes on the stage felt much longer. They felt shaky and extremely nervous when they waited for their turn behind the wings prior to their turn to dance. After the first show, participants expressed that they felt contentment and even joy when they danced on stage. This feeling was reinforced each time they performed on the stage.

David said,

It is really embarrassing at first because everyone is staring at you. The first show was definitely a nerve-racking experience. It was the first time I danced in front of that many people but the second one was a lot smoother. It is great to dance like that. Thinking back, I really missed performing on the stage.

Wilson experienced feelings of empowerment while dancing:

I worry a lot when I wait in the wings before getting on the stage. When I get on the stage, everything changes. Everything blends together smoothly and perfectly. I feel almost like empowered to do better. There is definitely more positive energy in the theatre coming from the audience, dancers around me, music, light, and the stage [Illus. 8.5].

Illus. 8.5. A male student dances "Sleepless Night" on the stage

Kyle revealed his post-performance reaction, which left him almost speechless:

> It's like ... Wah! I can't believe that I just did it. We did well and they [the audience] liked it. It feels good. It makes me think that I can dance. All these works [sweat, rehearsal time, costume, make-up] have been paid off!

Male dance students with more dance training and performing experience (connecting individuals) felt an instant connection the moment they stepped onto the stage. They tended to focus on movement and were less intimidated by the stage. In fact, most stated that they enjoyed every single second while performing and connecting with the audience. Jim talked about his moment on the stage:

> When I get on the stage, it is me and the audience with nothing else matters. In that moment, it is not a joyful feeling for me but a confident spirit electrifying throughout my entire body. I am happy to share this particular spirit and [I am sure that the] audience could feel it, too. It is like give and

Illus. 8.6. Students warm up in the gym
for the year-end dance performance

takes. Audiences give me applause and I give them my spirit through dance, which is what I enjoy the most in that moment [Illus. 8.7].

Michael enjoyed seeing audiences giving positive responses (such as applause) when the boys performed on stage. He was in a two-minute dance piece called "The Longest Time," a funny piece about the brevity of life and how we need to treasure each moment. Michael loved the story and the fact that the boys used movement to deliver the message:

> Before I got on stage, I felt shaky. It was definitely a big rush. It gives me goosebumps. It was [the] adrenaline rush you get from performing in front of a large group of audience members ... After our dance started, I felt so natural and relaxed. I liked our class piece because we make people laugh. That makes me happy. When I see the audience respond in that way, I know that I have achieved my goal.

Tom spoke about his experience of communicating with the audience through dance. As a second-year dance student, he was angry about how others in the public perceived male dancers. As a male

Illus. 8.7. Adolescent male dance students perform "It's Time" on stage

dance student performing on stage, he saw himself as a role model to reduce stereotypes:

> It is always special when dancing in front of audiences. I think that's what breaks the stereotypes: when people see me and other guys dancing together on stage. None of us have comprehensive training in dance but we are dancing on stage anyway. When my friends see that, I don't think they will think about dance the way they would have thought before ... They know who I am and they see I am doing something completely different and that makes a difference, I think. It's kind of fun to throw people off like that.

According to Abraham Maslow's (1943) hierarchy of needs, self-actualization is the pinnacle of human growth. Maslow describes this level as when a person's full potential is realized. The phrase "self-actualized performers" describes those who acknowledged that they accomplished something worthwhile while performing on the stage. A feeling of intrinsic reward is established by individuals themselves. These adolescent male dance students had the most dance training and performance experience compared to other males in the school. They were more accustomed to dancing in front of large audiences. They admitted that they only experienced nervousness occasionally at the beginning of the show. Once the show began, they were able to quickly adjust their mind and to focus on what lay ahead – dancing (Illus. 8.8).

Illus. 8.8. Adolescent male dance students show off their moves
before getting on stage

All of the students in this study expressed that when they were performing on stage, it felt like they were in their own world. They were
not thinking of the audience or others. They forgot who they were and
became who they wanted to be while dancing on the stage. They experienced the "flow" while performing, even the first-year students who
did not find that feeling in classes and rehearsals. That feeling matches
the results of Risner's (2009c) study, in which nearly all his research
participants chose performing as their reason for dancing. Dancing on
stage in front of an audience seemed to be a magical experience for
many young boys. When these adolescent male dancers got off the
stage after the show, they still felt jittery, but they also felt uplifted and
energized, to the extent that they wanted to do it again almost immediately. They found it really hard to sleep on the night of the performance because they were so "hyped-up." One of the students summa-
rized it:

It is just me – dancing. I don't have much things pounding on me during dance performances. I know that I am in control. My spirit, body, and mind all become one. Sometimes, it does become a blank as I don't refer [to] myself as who I am but who I am as a character on stage … During the performance night, I see myself as part of the puzzle or picture. I feel relaxed and comfortable. I know that stage is the place where I belong to, where I live, where I thrive, and where I am alive.

Eleanor Stubley (1995) discusses the relationship between the composer and the musician who is performing that particular composer's score. In *The Performer, the Score, the Work: Musical Performance and Transactional Reading*, Stubley refers to this working relationship as a "transactional event," in which the musician lives in and through his/her action while performing the composer's work. Similarly, these adolescent male dancers lived in and through their action – dancing – while performing a choreographer's work. They became characters who explored the world within and around, without being aware of it themselves; they created a dialectic interaction between the outside (audience) and the inside (themselves). In the process, they transformed their emotional and meaningful issues, moving them from themselves into other bodies. Their embodied movements revealed who they were or the characters they were attempting to portray. At that moment, these adolescent male dancers knew that they had reached their full potential, or "flow," and they enjoyed it tremendously.

9

Dancing Through Our Lives

These adolescent male dance students reminded me of who I was 20 years ago, having an interest in dance but not committed to it, enjoying performing in front of people but reluctant to speak about dance in public, thriving in a female-dominated profession but often entertaining thoughts of quitting. The students and I danced in two different worlds in terms of geographic location, time, culture, and political environment, yet what we went through was quite similar. We all experienced pain and fame, shame and pride while dancing, although the length of time we spent in dance was different, ranging from a few months to several years for the boys, whereas mine is still ongoing. Through this research and my own experience, I have concluded that adolescent male dancers' presence in dance is constantly challenged by internal and external pressures that threaten the existence of males in dance.

What made me and other boys stay in dance? For years, I questioned myself and searched for answers with little success. It was only when I had nearly completed this book that I could put the puzzle together. To survive in dance during the adolescent years, youths need a lot of support. Positive attributions or factors such as peer influence, a sense of community, and a feeling of "flow" are some of the reasons that the adolescents in my study and I were able to keep from becoming "refugees" from dance. I use the term "refugees" to describe those males who drop out of dance at an early stage. Many Rosedale boys pointed to their positive feelings while dancing. One of the boys said that "nobody is being judged or criticized for height, weight, body shape, or level of dance skills." While dancing, we tend not to think about unpleasant past experiences and we focus on what we are doing at present – dancing – in which we experience "flow" and excitement. Was that the reason we chose to dance in the first place? Not really. Few of us were told prior to our commitment in dance that this sense of happiness would occur. Yet this study found that adolescent males can experience the same joy in dancing as those males who have trained and danced in professional and semi-professional settings for decades.

The all-boys dance class was essential for attracting adolescent males to dance and keeping them in it. The creation of an all-boys dance class certainly increased the popularity of dance among males at Rosedale and decreased anxiety and fear for those who might not have wanted to take dance in the first place. Many boys in this study had no previous dance training background, and they chose dance when an all-boys class became an option on the course selection sheet. Nevertheless, this book does not undermine the importance of mixed-gender dance classes. It simply points out that having the option of an all-boys dance class in high schools can be an effective way to get more males to sign up for dance classes.

This study generates a list of strategies to attract and retain adolescent males in dance. The list includes movement-based games, field trips, weightlifting opportunities, YouTube or other video sharing, the integration of technology in dance classes, rapport with teachers, and even a "swimming pool ballet" approach, which Rosedale Heights offered once or twice as an end-of-year "adventure" for students. The book also highlights that teaching dance to young males requires giving or offering immediate incentives and using creative approaches. To some boys in this study, having access to the weightlifting or fitness room once a month was a good reason to take dance. The inclusion of the fitness room option for the dance class is not written directly in the dance curriculum. However, it could be interpreted that such activities (visiting the weightlifting room and using fitness facilities) enhance what they learn in dance classes. In the revised *The Arts: The Ontario Curriculum, Grades 9 and 10* (2010), it states, "By the end of this course [dance], students will demonstrate an understanding of the importance of a positive body image and a healthy lifestyle to their learning in dance"; dance students are also required to understand the "nature and function of the skeletal/muscular system in relation to the physiology of movement" (p. 56).

For other adolescent male dancers, working out with popular music seemed to be a fun thing to do. "Getting a workout and earning a high school credit at the same time is a no-brainer choice for me," one boy said in class. In the past few years, there had been a growing trend at Rosedale of senior students (17 to 19 years old) deciding to take dance.

These boys had often fulfilled high school requirements (earned all of their required credits) but decided to take an extra year in high school for various reasons. Some of these older boys described dance as a "once-in-a-lifetime adventure." One senior boy wrote in his reflection,

> Dancing in the water [swimming pool] is like a miracle. Jumping in the water becomes effortless and turning, kicking [straight] legs up are much harder than I do in the studio. Suddenly, those abstract and confusing terms that I heard from science and physics classes come to light through my body. I would have never imagined doing this in dance class. Big jumps from the spring board make me feel like a bird.

Did swimming pool ballet classes affect their decision to take dance? Did popular music make them want to dance? I could not confirm because these few students were seniors in the school and many were heading to university or to the workplace. There was no time for follow-up interviews on how senior high school students thought about dance. Nevertheless, pool ballet and popular music certainly were among those aspects to which they attributed their positive experience in dance.

Meanwhile, when it came to teaching junior males at Rosedale (grades 9 and 10), using different teaching strategies proved to be effective. The light-hearted classroom atmosphere, mutual respect, and gradual introduction to dance steps were frequently commented on by junior dance males. In contrast, these strategies were the opposite of what I had gone through in my own dance training. My early dance training during my adolescent years was filled with rules, compliance, harsh criticism, and even physical abuse. In such an extreme high-pressured environment, I became quite resentful towards dance. Looking at dance training from a different angle, would a light-hearted and respectful approach work in professional and semi-professional dance training institutions? That could be an interesting topic to explore. But these adolescent males at Rosedale chose dance because they were interested and dance was available to them. Their decision to take dance was driven by curiosity and immediate incentives (music, fitness, high school credit). These immediate incentives or tangible rewards proved to be effective in attracting adolescent males to dance.

In my case, immediate incentives were non-existent, especially at the early dance training stage. Unlike these adolescent males, I did not have an option to choose what I wanted to do when I was an adolescent. When I grew up, there was a culture in China that kids had to learn something in addition to regular schooling. Similar to the hockey culture in eastern Canada, many kids in my hometown focused on arts and sports. Although none of my parents or relatives knew anything about the arts, particularly dance, they helped me make the decision to study dance. My brother, on the other hand, was pushed into music (learning to play the oboe) a few years later. It all started with good intentions that regular school education was not enough and that something else had to be added to the "survival list." According to my parents, that something meant learning a skill that was not overwhelmingly popular. The goal was to maximize our opportunity to succeed. Years later, their unscientific but common-sense-based bet proved to be right. I become a successful male in dance and my brother, who learned an unfamiliar instrument, became one of the top oboe players in China.

Dance in my life has been a mixture of love and hate. As I stated in the beginning of this chapter, dance has helped me achieve so much in life, but it also gave me unsettled moments filled with self-doubt, pressure, and sadness. What makes me keep going? To be more specific, what makes me stay in dance? Both the English idiom "practice makes perfect" and the Chinese version of "you get what you pay for" best describe my journey in dance. On the one hand, I have to credit my (as well as my parents') perseverance and character trait of not easily giving up, which helped me stay in dance. On the other hand, long-term rewards from my dance training, such as scholarships, performance opportunities, touring, and other career opportunities, further convinced me to continue. I did not have the same immediate incentives as the adolescent male dance students enjoyed at Rosedale though. Instead, competition, pressure, and high expectations were a daily presence during my early dance training. Looking back, I am glad that I have invested time, energy, and patience in dance. If I had ever followed through on my thought of quitting dance, I would never have gotten into the elite dance school, become an army officer, and obtained my academic degrees. I would have never left Harbin, studied in Hong Kong, and immigrated to Canada. Personally, I have benefited tremendously from being a male in dance. I am thriving in this profession, but how can I share my stories and experiences with other males who might want to pursue dance as a career or who simply want to take dance? There seems to be so much that we can do to promote dance among adolescent males. Nothing will change, though, without deciding to start somewhere. Strategically, I believe that the promotion of physical health, or what I would like to call "bodily intelligence," can be a good starting point.

I have always told my students that the body is more intelligent than the mind. Long before we can logically organize our thoughts and are able to speak properly, we know how to move our body. Elders from different parts of the world would likely describe it spiritually, as seen in Indian and Greek mythologies. I see it as dance. We "dance" at birth, at parties, on vacation, and at a variety of events. Dance is a popular activity among younger kids, both boys and girls, who usually react to their moods, their emotions, and music with all kinds of bodily or gestural expressions. However, as kids get older, they start to refrain from expressing happiness and excitement through their body. They do that because they see what adults do. As adults, male and female, we no longer jump in thrill when we get a pay raise or enjoy a movie, as we would have done when we were young. In many places, particularly in the West, we tend to discourage boys from taking dance because of who we are, what we do, and what our friends do. We are inclined to "follow" others, sometimes willingly and sometimes not, and we would like our children to do the same – to "fit in." Achieving high marks in literacy and mathematics becomes a high priority among parents once their children begin formal schooling. Meanwhile, the number of boys in dance decreases drastically starting from grade 1 (six years old). Young boys are more likely to follow their friends' interests such as sports and electronic games, apart from their schoolwork. In a sense we indirectly drive boys out of dance, and so do boys themselves. As time goes by, we lose the passion and joy of using our body to express, communicate, and celebrate. I always use a "body is smarter than mind" story in my dance class. I say, "Everyone would retrieve their hands immediately when touching something hot. In such a situation, the person would not check the temperature, the object, nor which part of the hand got burned. They just react to the heat intuitively – pulling back their hands quickly." That is one example of how the body reacts faster than the mind. I also share this with dance students: "Over the years, I have learned to listen to my body, then process in my mind before taking further action. Whenever I feel tired, pressured, stressed, and frustrated, I go and take a dance class to let my body calm down. In the midst of sweat and moving through space, my thoughts get reorganized and my mind stays focused." Dance to me is a therapeutic process and it goes much deeper than just the physical exercise. A colleague used to argue with me about this theory and tried to convince me to simply lay down, rest, and reflect. Well, it never works for me; my thoughts would go wild and I would become even more agitated. In a dance class, I have to pay undivided attention to what the instructor says. I listen to the music, count the rhythm, execute certain moves and steps on the right tempo, travel in, out, and through a dance space without hitting others, and the list goes on. It would seem that this is a confusing and chaotic scene, but once the whole body and mind work together, a miracle happens. The body is much more capable of juggling many different things at the same time than one would imagine. In this study, adolescent males who had taken dance for two years or longer shared similar comments in their reflections and through interviews. Many were grateful for choosing dance, and they credited dance for their balanced development in physical and mental intelligence. If we consider the benefits for the body of one year of dance training, as suggested by junior dance students in this study, two years in dance was definitely a milestone at which boys began to experience the fruits of their labour. These senior boys gained a much deeper understanding of what dance is, how dance functions in society, and how it can be beneficial in their lives. Dance cultivated these boys' body intelligence so they lived, breathed, and enjoyed their life in a much more profound way.

Although there seems to be greater acceptance of males in dance today – as seen in these boys' responses, particularly among senior males – the stereotype of dance as not being a legitimate subject of study for boys persisted in many of their minds. By participating in dance, these boys broke some of the stereotypes in their own thinking, and for some, it was to the extent that they were considering dance professionally. Despite their attitude change and the fact that they were able to influence other boys' decisions to try dance, some socially constructed stereotypical thinking remained deeply embedded. For example, many boys continued to refer to dance as a "non-academic" or "irregular" subject, inferior to subjects such as math, science, and English. This was particularly obvious when they discussed dance during the first few months of dancing. It took some time for the boys to see dance as a form of literacy, in which and through which they could express, create, and communicate. Many adolescent males are blocked by a socially constructed presumption that dance is a girly activity, a type of entertainment, waste of time, or inferior to other subjects. It may be partially due to the lack of dance activities or creative movement–based classes at the elementary level. Then here is the question: How can dance be promoted at the elementary level? To solely depend on elementary school teachers to expand the scale of dance education is simply unrealistic. Multiple levels of administration are needed to help nurture elementary schools' dance programs. That includes school boards, universities with dance programs, institutions that grant teaching degrees, professional dance artists, high school dance educators/curriculum instructors, and curriculum policy designers.

Many school boards in Canada provide two to four professional development (PD) days for teachers during each school year. Before each PD day, teachers identify areas of improvement in terms of teaching and learning. They present a list of interests to the PD-day organizer, who is usually a regular teacher or a curriculum leader (lead teacher) at the school. This lead teacher surveys other teachers to get a general consensus about what should be included on PD days. For instance, because of teachers' requests, many PD days at Toronto District School Board schools in recent years have focused on implementing technology in classrooms.

Dance is a subject area at both elementary and secondary levels. High schools find it easier to offer dance classes because teachers are more specialized and can usually focus on delivering their subject areas. On the other hand, many elementary school teachers do not teach dance in their classroom because they are "general classroom teachers" and have to cover all subjects: language arts, math, science, and others. Dance is often overlooked because it is not considered a "core subject." Many elementary classroom teachers superficially assign a mark under dance on the report card, even though they did little or sometimes no dance activities during the school year. Instead, elementary school teachers could request a basic dance workshop to be offered on their professional development dates. Dance workshops should ideally be delivered in the school, not in a dance studio, as many schools do not have a proper dance studio. This way, elementary school teachers could have a first-hand experience in how to teach dance in a place they are familiar with and working with the space and resources that they have. It is worth pointing out that in almost all Canadian schools, there is an auditorium, an indoor gym, or an empty classroom which could be designated as a "dance room."

What kind of dance would be most suitable for elementary schools? It varies according to the location of the school, socio-economic environment, and teachers' backgrounds. Within this study, some students mentioned taking folk dance and creative movement–based workshops in the past. Personally, I find folk dance and creative movement–based dance classes are more suitable for elementary school teachers. Both dance styles require little or no dance experience or training. Workshop presenters could be a teacher with a dance background or a dance artist who is familiar with teaching dance to younger kids in a school environment. Working for the largest school board in Canada (TDSB), I observed how dance workshops can change elementary teachers' views on dance education. Bringing effective dance workshops to elementary classroom teachers demystifies dance education and encourages classroom teachers to use dance for integration (math and language arts), collaboration (skills sharing among teachers), and school engagement (practice and performance among students).

Elements for effective dance workshops for elementary school teachers include easy adaptation, little or no resources required, and a genderless approach (males and females learn the same movements). It is always preferable that workshop leaders share a music piece, present a slideshow covering a brief history of a particular dance form, and lead a simple and short dance routine. A post-workshop sharing session is welcome to help teachers brainstorm multiple ways to teach the same dance to different levels, in various settings, and to diverse groups. These crash-course-style dance workshops are quite effective in terms of providing what general classroom teachers need (ideas and basic steps), what they have to know (brief history), and how they are to teach (methods). In my previous experience as a dance workshop leader, I noticed that teachers in this kind of workshop sometimes commented on how they successfully integrated dance into other subject areas, including language arts (dance workshop reflection), math (fractions, addition, subtraction), and social studies (culture, race, and character). Dance workshops for elementary schools on PD days would encourage general classroom teachers to embrace dance in their classroom.

Universities, especially those with dance programs and faculties that grant a teaching degree, could also play an important role in promoting dance among males in schools. For instance, York University in Toronto has the largest dance program in Canada, with nearly 300 students in different degree programs. York's dance program has revised and expanded its curriculum to focus on dance research (master's and doctorate studies), dance choreography/performance (bachelor of fine arts), and dance education (concurrent degree program with the Faculty of Education). Students in the concurrent program (bachelor of fine arts and bachelor of education) have to take at least one full year of education-related courses before obtaining their joint degrees, in addition to completing their four-year study in a subject area. With a dance background and multidimensional approach (theory and practical teaching methods), they have an edge in terms of attracting adolescent males to dance. There is usually a student-body-based dance company within the university dance program. In recent years, the York Dance Ensemble[1] (YDE), with selected dance major students, has periodically visited public schools in the province of Ontario. Their in-school performances are well received by schools, especially those located in less affluent neighbourhoods, where students cannot afford to attend live dance performances. As a researcher and former dance teacher in public schools, I would recommend such performances be held in more schools and in a wider range. Currently YDE showcases their works in specialized schools where dance is offered. I would argue such programs should bring dance performance to as many schools as possible, particularly to elementary schools to expose younger kids to dance.

Bringing dance performance/workshops to schools creates a positive image among younger students, especially students who have limited exposure to dance. Many of the YDE performers are adolescents themselves, as some first-year undergraduate students can be as young as 16 or 17 years old if they have skipped grades or if their birthday is early in the calendar year. The ensemble dance pieces are usually choreographed by faculty members, guest artists, and students themselves. It is likely that students sitting in the audience can relate to the performers because of age similarities. This becomes particularly clear when post-performance dance workshops take place. After the performance, university dance students talk about their experience in dance training, performance, and studies. They answer questions about the performance and they also lead dance workshops. In particular, the few male university dance students often receive more attention, and they are frequently asked why they chose to study dance in the first place. In a sense, the workshop section demystifies dance, especially abstract modern dance, among public school students. It also provides another angle for male students in public schools to look at dance more positively, by seeing other males dancing. Many public school students, particularly males, have limited exposure to dance performance for many reasons. University dance students performing in public schools promotes dance among students, both males and females.

---

1 The York Dance Ensemble (York University, 2016) is the resident company of the Department of Dance. Since 1988, the YDE has been providing upper-level dancers, choreographers, musicians, and production crews with pre-professional experience creating, producing, performing, and touring in a company setting. Students experience a range of performance venues, from galleries to schools and other alternative settings.

Whereas some universities such as York acknowledge the importance of dance and dance education by taking their dance productions to public schools, the vast majority of universities in Ontario, which have no dance program, provide little or no support in this regard. The University of Toronto (U of T), one of the most reputable universities in Canada, has more than 80,000 students (a 2014 figure). Ontario Institute for Studies in Education (OISE), U of T's education centre, is the largest teacher training institution in the province of Ontario. It provides little support for teaching dance in schools or for meeting dance curriculum expectations to its teacher-candidates (student-teachers in teacher certification programs). OISE offers a few dance workshops to over 1,000 teacher-candidates during their two-year certification program. None of OISE's faculty members have a dance background, however, which means the workshops are usually led by dance instructors who might not be familiar with the dance curriculum or classroom management, nor do they necessarily have the ability to teach dance effectively in regular classrooms. Meanwhile, literacy, math, science, and even music have been covered extensively. When compared to all curriculum subjects, dance is not treated fairly, particularly when considering that OISE's strategic plan for 2011–15 proclaims that the institution is "proud of their history and guided by their commitment to equity and social justice" (Ontario Institute for Studies in Education of the University of Toronto, 2014).

Professional dance companies and dance artists are crucial in promoting dance and gender equity in dance. In recent years, a growing number of dance organizations in Toronto have recognized the importance of creating an education network or having some kind of outreach program. National Ballet of Canada, Ballet Jörgen, Opera Atelier, Kaeja d'Dance, Toronto Dance Theatre, and many others have been cultivating their audience base through initiatives based on dance education. Canada's National Ballet School offers associate dance programs that allow boys and girls, ages 6 to 17, to participate in after-school and weekend dance classes throughout the year. National Ballet of Canada provides free company tours to Ontario public schools. Ballet Jörgen's company dancers travel via plane, bus, and van across Ontario and the rest of Canada to showcase their dance work in schools and communities. This company is particularly interesting to watch because many of the male dancers come from diverse ethnic backgrounds (such as Cuban, Japanese, and Chinese). Opera Atelier invites hundreds of public school students to attend their week-long dance event, which covers baroque dance history, music in the early sixteenth and seventeenth centuries, prop making, costume design, and a dance workshop. At the end, students are invited to watch a dress rehearsal of the company's latest production free of charge. Toronto Dance Theatre (TDT) invites public school students to their facility to watch a dance performance, followed by a dance workshop, then a Q&A session. TDT provides students with some basic information on contemporary dance and also challenges them to think and reflect on what they have just seen on stage. Dance companies' efforts and time are not wasted, as one of the participants in the research for this book admitted that he was inspired by a ballet performance. After high school, he continued his dance training and eventually became a professional dancer with Opera Atelier.

Equally as important as these initiatives by dance companies are independent dance artists, who also have a positive impact on school dance programs. Their programs are usually small in size, range from one to half a dozen dancers, and they are mobile in terms of travelling to different schools. Nonetheless, this research found that not many professional dance artists in Ontario know that they can apply for government subsidies from the Ontario Arts Council and the Canada Council for the Arts to bring their performance to schools. Both organizations provide a number of options for dance artists, including financial assistance for individual dance artists to travel locally, nationally, and even internationally. For example, interested dance artists could get professional advice from other dance experts and participate in the Shared Payment program, where the government provides 80 per cent of the cost of a dance workshop/performance while the school pays only 20 per cent. It alleviates the financial pressure for many of the public schools, which usually cannot afford to pay the entire cost. These smaller-scale dance workshops and performances can sometimes create a big impact on how public school students think about dance. Small dance companies offer more diverse and popular dance styles to students, are more mobile (with fewer performers), and are not usually too picky about the performance space. Some participants in the study did mention that seeing dance performances and participating in dance workshops in their school made them want to learn dance. That was especially evident when the dance performance was based on hip hop or jazz.

High schools, especially those with dance programs, can also help elementary schools develop dance programs. High school dance educators usually have more resources for teaching dance, and they can certainly assist their elementary colleagues in initiating dance activities. Dance educators in Earl Haig Secondary School's Claude Watson Arts Program,

Rosedale Heights School of the Arts, and David Suzuki Secondary School in Mississauga, among others, have been working tirelessly in recent years in this regard. These dance educators share their teaching resources, promote dance programs among junior high school students, and bring dance performances to elementary schools. Some high schools even organize dance festivals for similar goals. Recently, a group of high school teachers from London District Catholic School Board hosted a Dance Fest among primary, junior, and intermediate schools in London, Ontario. Their mission statement says,

> Dance Fest is an opportunity for teachers and their students to share and celebrate dancing. Dance Fest is not a competitive situation, but rather an opportunity for an entire class of children to participate in a function designed to provide an extension to the dance taught in the instructional program. Dance Fest serves as a vehicle through which "dance ideas" can be shared in an atmosphere of joy and celebration. There is also an opportunity to integrate the Physical Education Curriculum with the Arts Curriculum. (London District Catholic School Board, 2014)

High school teachers in the London area did more than just bring dance performances to elementary schools. They got elementary teachers involved in the dance festival and they also extended their invitation to physical education and regular classroom teachers. Similar initiatives also took place through Toronto District School Board, the largest school board in Canada. One such event, Dare2Create 2014, was a collaborative event to promote dance, drama, media arts, and visual arts in almost 600 schools.

> Dare2Create 2014 is the first annual system-wide celebration of dance, drama, media arts and visual arts in the TDSB. The festival runs from May 2 to June 10 in schools, communities, galleries, and performing arts venues around Toronto. Students, teachers, and artists will come together as a community to create, celebrate, and learn together. The theme of the festival is a celebration of student voice, creativity, and our city stories. (TDSB, 2014)

According to TDSB's website, Dare2Create 2014 attracted more than 5,000 students participating in all kinds of school-based and community-based events. Though female dancers far outnumbered male dancers, the aforementioned events provided an opportunity for males to see and meet other male dancers of similar ages, backgrounds, and skills. As more festivals and arts events featuring dance are organized, it becomes more likely that adolescent males will view dance positively and be willing to participate. More urgently, public schools should consider offering all-boys dance classes to encourage more males to take dance and to ease their initial struggles in getting involved in dance. To help boys become interested in dance, school administration at the elementary level needs to promote dance by inviting dance artists to teach dance in schools. Teachers, especially males who have had dance experience, would be ideal candidates for such initiatives.

Although high school seems to be a great place to launch dance programs because teenage students have the opportunity to pick their elective courses, educators cannot take this for granted. Currently, many high schools in the province of Ontario do not offer dance courses. Even in specialized arts schools, for instance, where dance might appear as an option on the course selection sheet, adolescent males are not necessarily going to choose to enrol in dance. Some arts schools in Toronto witness low enrolment of male dance students. This research shows that few adolescent males admitted that they find it easier to take dance at an arts-focused school, which proves that even in an environment that appears to support and encourage dance for all students, there are still great barriers to adolescent males freely opting for dance. This finding is not surprising when one considers the place of dance in the Canadian society. For many people in the public, dance is often perceived as entertainment while math and science, for instance, improve standards of living. To alter this perception of dance, there needs to be involvement in promoting dance by higher-level government officials and institutions. For instance, agencies that fund the arts (e.g., the Canada Council for the Arts and the Toronto Arts Council) should create scholarships/ financial assistance to support beginner males in dance. It could be partial financial support for male dance students who want to pursue dance after high school or want to become teachers. One boy in this study who eventually became a professional dancer admitted that it was quite a struggle to pursue dance as a career. After high school, he attended postsecondary dance training at Canada's National Ballet School with his mother's financial support. He had to take additional classes to make his dance dream come true and had to keep a part-time job just to be able to "stay in the game."

Several boys in this study shared that within certain cultures and ethnic groups, dance in general (e.g., Ukrainian dance) or a particular dance form (e.g., hip hop) is acceptable for males. In other words, young males are more likely to see certain dance forms as a more "legitimate" activity and will be more likely to give it a try. This finding has many implications. For schools with a dominant ethnic group, in example, introducing adolescent boys to dance by starting with certain cultural dance forms could be better received as community-building or as passing on a part of their heritage rather than simply learning to dance. If other dance forms such as krump and hip hop were included in training, this could become challenging for educators, especially since many may not feel comfortable teaching a style of dance that they are not familiar with. Also, popular dance forms evolve so quickly that educators have to constantly "catch up," which might not be realistic. A solution could be found within the student body or school community: someone with a background in that dance form could be invited to initiate dance workshops/clubs. In this case, both teachers and students can learn together. Ethnic and popular dance styles work well in both arts-focused and non-arts-focused schools as they bring students together, whether they are male, female, beginner, or advanced dance students. Queen Victoria Public School (kindergarten to grade 6) in Toronto offers an example of such an initiative. According to school enrolment information from 2014, close to 80 per cent of its 760 students spoke a primary language other than English, and the vast majority of students and their families were of Southeast Asian background (Queen Victoria Public School, 2014). Each year, principals at the school organize events for the Festival of Light – Divali, which is a prominent Hindu festival celebrated by many Southeast Asians. During the festival, students participate in school activities, and dance is one of the highlights. After years of running the festival, many classroom teachers have gotten to know the culture, traditions, costumes, and even basic dance steps. At the dance performance, teachers as well as students wear saris (female Indian dress) and sarongs (male cloth worn by those from South Asia, Southeast Asia, the Arabian peninsula, and the Pacific Islands). They dance around the hallway and on the stage for the main performance. It is important to note that gender in dance is not an issue, as males and females, students, teachers, caretakers, and principals are all involved.

Another example is how a popular dance, hip hop, attracts males to dance. At Rosedale Heights School of the Arts, a hip hop club used to be run by a dance teacher, but after the club's leadership was transferred to senior dance students, the participant numbers exploded. At the time of the study, twice a week at lunchtime for half an hour, more than 60 students flooded into the biggest dance room to practice their cool moves.

Many of these students were not taking dance in school, but they enjoyed the atmosphere in the hip hop club. Some males came to the club to experience the joy and to sweat, and a few subsequently decided to sign up for a dance class. These young dancers were committed, came in with proper dress, and worked really hard for the final performance. The hip hop club's dance is usually one of the most popular dance pieces in a dance night performance.

Senior male dance students who share their insights about dance help beginning male dancers understand the different stages they may go through when taking dance. Male dance students are informed right at the beginning that thoughts of quitting are normal because, as the minority, they might feel alone and sometimes they cannot reference their actions against those of other boys who do not dance. Online blogging and classroom reflection work really well in this sense because boys share their experience in dance without identifying themselves. Previous discussions are kept online for new male dance students to read and share with others. In this study, students came with different dance backgrounds. Some boys were slightly more experienced because they took dance the year before. That became an advantage in the all-boys dance class. Students who continued to take dance helped and supported juniors with difficult movements or routines. They acted like "big brothers" and cultivated a friendly community. Their actions helped many beginner male dance students overcome the initial challenges. In return, these senior male dance students felt accomplished and were more likely to stay in dance.

This study also showed that almost all of the adolescent male dance students who tried dance, overcame the initial challenges, and stayed for a period of time were able to attain some degree of "flow." Hence, the key strategy is to first provide more adolescent boys with opportunities to participate in dance classes and minimize the initial stress. Ethnic and hip hop dance forms are great ways to get boys interested in dance, and sharing insights with other males in dance sustains that interest. A collaborative approach between physical education teachers and dance instructors could be a way to try this idea. It is not uncommon for professional athletes to refine their performance by taking dance classes. Thus, it may not be far-fetched to suggest that physical education classes should have a mandatory unit for students to learn dance. This idea would allow more adolescent boys to experience dance in what may seem to them a more "legitimate" setting and with a more "legitimate" purpose. While dancing, adolescent males can see similarities and be able to make connections between these two subjects. In order to make the collaboration happen, physical education teachers, dance educators, and school administrators need to be supportive and engaged in timetabling and planning logistics. Such initiatives can take place in both arts-focused and non-arts-focused schools to create a sustainable change in the attitudes of adolescent boys towards dance.

We have discussed at length the realities of the adolescent male dancers in this study – the challenges they face and the "flow" that many experienced. It is noteworthy that although adolescent males generally face tremendous social and developmental obstacles, many are not shaken in their determination to dance once they have persevered for a certain time. Regardless of whether these adolescent males continue to dance in the future, it is certain that they now have a completely different understanding of dance and they are less likely to reject males in dance when they grow older. Similar to the journey that I went through when I was a dance student, these young males may one day become advocates for other males who might give dance a try. I strongly believe that dance can function as a vehicle in which and through which adolescent male dance students can express themselves and learn; become shaped and reshaped in their thinking, formed and reformed in their beliefs; and discover who they are and what they want to be in the future. I speak from my own life, without wishing my patterns on the youth. But my dreams can be shared. One of my students found the words to explain his dancing life, and in many respects, my life as well:

> Taking dance in high school gives me a balance between my body and my mind. It is a fact that most people tend to ignore in their lives. It is great thinking back in old times of ballet when people see a "literal bond" between these two. People believe that in order to balance your physical body, you have to maintain a clear mind. Taking ballet helps me think, react, and behave more logically and responsibly. It teaches me how to be in touch with myself as well as understand others through movements. Even more than that is the way I have to live in dance, the way I have to push myself, and the way I fight for my survival in dance. That makes my life unique and, to me, meaningful.

Appendix
Video Documentary on Adolescent Male Dance Students

I have created an interpretative documentary film to enhance the authenticity, accessibility, visibility, and comprehensibility of this research. I call it an interpretative documentary film because my interpretation includes selecting, sequencing, and organizing the raw data into this documentary film. It comes in three versions (1 minute, 10 minutes, and 60 minutes) to meet different needs. You can view the videos on YouTube:

One-minute trailer: https://youtu.be/t8etNl84G2Y

Ten-minute film: https://youtu.be/9K-nUlqkLqQ

Sixty-minute film: https://youtu.be/h56bZNFaqkI

The 1-minute trailer gives readers an introduction to the research. It shows the highlights of the 60-minute documentary by flashing through still images and short video and audio clips. The full-length documentary (60 minutes) serves many purposes. It is a condensed version of all the data, which includes videotaping, audiotaping, field notes, detailed interviews, classes, rehearsals, and performances. During the research, Margaret Bailey (the camera grip) and I gathered a substantial amount of video material (over 50 hours), including jazz, modern, and ballet classes, rehearsals, studio warm-ups, putting on make-up, auditions, and different performances both inside and outside the school. The scenes were sorted and condensed to provide viewers with comprehensive coverage of the study. Since videotaping took place over the entire school year, it documented the changing attitudes that the students had towards dance at different times. In the full-length version, viewers can also see the technical advancement that these adolescent males made in dance over time.

This documentary serves as a meaningful and powerful instrument to gain a better understanding of the classroom situation, the relationship between students and teacher, the learning environment, the progression of the boys' technique, their attitude towards dance over time, and interactions among the boys themselves. As a dance teacher, I knew that solely depending on interviews, classroom observations, and field notes was far from sufficient for capturing the energy and authenticity of the all-boys dance class. Because of the nature of the research topic (dance) and its pace, visual data (videotaping) in addition to textual data provides more accuracy. This film gives adolescent male dance students a voice and lets them speak for themselves and be themselves.

This documentary adds more power and meaning than quoting statements of the study participants in textual form. The film presents concrete and detailed evidence to support as well as enliven my findings. It provides evidence about the process of teaching young males to dance in a high school situation. It also allows for reflection for me as a dance educator and for the students. I sincerely hope that my work (book and film) will inspire other educators to rethink their teaching concerning adolescent males in dance and to challenge the socially constructed notion that dance is only for entertainment.

References

Aalten, A. (1997). Performing the body, creating culture. *European Journal of Women's Studies, 4*(2), 197–215. http://dx.doi.org/10.1177/135050689700400205

Acker, S. (1994). *Gendered education: Sociological reflections on women, teaching and feminism.* Milton Keynes, UK: Open University Press.

Acocella, J.R. (1995, 23 April). Real men don't point their feet. *Village Voice*, p. 78.

Adler, A.H.W. (2002). A case study of boys' experiences of singing in school (Unpublished doctoral dissertation). University of Toronto.

Agrelo, M. (Director & Producer), & Sewell, A. (Producer). (2005, 13 May). *Mad hot ballroom* [Motion picture]. United States: Paramount Vantage.

Anderson, E. (2010). *Inclusive Masculinity: The Changing Nature of Masculinities.* New York, NY: Routledge.

The arts: The Ontario curriculum, grades 9 and 10. (2010). [Toronto, ON]: Ministry of Education. Retrieved from http://www.edu.gov.on.ca/eng/curriculum/secondary/arts910curr2010.pdf

The arts: The Ontario curriculum, grades 11 and 12. (2010). [Toronto, ON]: Ministry of Education. Retrieved from http://www.edu.gov.on.ca/eng/curriculum/secondary/arts1112curr2010.pdf

Baranowski, T. (1992). Assessment, prevalence, and cardiovascular benefits of physical activity and fitness in youth. *Medical Science Sports & Exercise, 24*(6), 237–47.

Barone, T., & Eisner, E.W. (1997). Arts-based educational research. In R.M. Jaeger (Ed.), *Complementary methods for research in education* (2nd ed.), (72–116). Washington, DC: American Educational Research Association.

Benoit, A.M. (2000, 14 November). Boys have numbers down male dance pupils are scarce, but instructors hope a new film will persuade more of them to try. *Chicago Tribune*, p. E1.

Berger, A.J. (2003). Dance & masculinity: Shifting social constructions of gender (Unpublished master's thesis). Boston College, Massachusetts.

Bev, D. (2001). Boys can dance. *The Boys in Schools Bulletin, 4*(3), 42–5. Retrieved from http://www.newcastle.edu.au/__data/assets/pdf_file/0005/66938/ BiSB_2001_vol-4_no-3.pdf

Bleakley, E.W., & Brennan, D.A. (2008). Physical education and sport education in Northern Ireland. In G. Klein & K. Hardman (Eds.), *Physical education and sport education in the European Union* (298–314). Paris: Edition Revue EPS.

Blount, J.M. (2000). Spinsters, bachelors, and other gender transgressors in school employment, 1850–1990. *Review of Educational Research, 70*(1), 83–101. http://rer.sagepub.com/content/70/1/83.full.pdf

Bond, K.E. (1994). How "wild things" tamed gender distinctions. *JOPERD – Journal of Physical Education, Recreation & Dance, 65*(2), 28–33. http://dx.doi .org/10.1080/07303084.1994.10606851

Bond, K.E., & Stinson, S.W. (2000–1). "I feel like I'm going to take off!": Young people's experiences of the superordinary in dance. *Dance Research Journal, 32*(2), 52–87. http://dx.doi.org/10.2307/1477981

Booth, D. (2002). *Even hockey players read: Boys and reading.* Markham, ON: Pembroke Publishers.

Brennan, D. (1993). Adolescent girls and disco dancing. *Body Matters: Leisure Image and Lifestyles, 47*, 6–11.

Brennan, D. (1996). Dance in the Northern Ireland physical education curriculum. *Women's Studies International Forum, 19*(5), 493–503. http:// dx.doi.org/10.1016/0277-5395(96)00050-7. Retrieved from http://www .sciencedirect.com/science/article/pii/0277539596000507

Burt, R. (1995). *The male dancer: Bodies, spectacle, sexualities.* London, UK: Routledge. http://dx.doi.org/10.4324/9780203359761

Burt, R. (1998). *Alien bodies: Representations of modernity, "race," and nation in early modern dance.* London, UK: Routledge.

Burt, R. (2007). *The male dancer: Bodies, spectacle, sexualities* (2nd ed.). London, UK: Routledge.

Carroll, T.G. (2000). If we didn't have the schools we have today, would we create the schools we have today? *Education, 1*(1), 117–40.

Citron, P. (2005a, 22 August). Ffida best of the best. *The Globe and Mail,* p. R3.

Citron, P. (2005b, 23 August). New steps for international dance fest. *The Globe and Mail,* p. R4.

Cole, A.L., & Knowles, J.G. (Eds.). (2000). *Researching teaching: Exploring teacher development through reflexive inquiry.* Boston, MA: Allyn and Bacon.

Connell, R. (1989). Cool guys, swots and wimps: The interplay of masculinity and education. *Oxford Review of Education, 15*(3), 291–303. http://dx.doi .org/10.1080/0305498890150309

Connell, R. (1993). *Schools and social justice.* London, UK: Pluto Press.

Connell, R. (1995). *Masculinities.* Crows Nest, Australia: Allen and Unwin.

Cook, M. (2008, 17 July). American footballers do ballet! BBC London. Retrieved from http://www.bbc.co.uk/london/content/articles/2008/07/17/greenwich_americanfootball_feature.shtml

Crawford, J.R. (1994). Encouraging male participation in dance. *JOPERD – Journal of Physical Education, Recreation & Dance, 65*(2), 40–3.

Csikszentmihalyi, M. (1990). *Flow: The psychology of optimal experience.* New York, NY: Harper & Row.

d'Amboise, J., & Seham, J. (1994). *National dance institute's 1994/1995 school year program.* Manuscript in preparation.

Deluzio, J. (1998). *Dance and physical education.* Manuscript in preparation.

Deluzio, J. (2009). *Today's parents, teachers, artists, and administrators: Keep dance in schools.* Manuscript in preparation.

DeMarco, T., & Sidney, K. (1989). Enhancing children's participation in physical activity. *Journal of School Health, 59*(8), 337–40. http://dx.doi.org/10.1111/j.1746-1561.1989.tb04739.x

Desmond, J.C. (1993). Embodying difference: Issues in dance and cultural studies. *Cultural Critique, 26,* 33–63. http://dx.doi.org/10.2307/1354455

Desmond, J.C. (2001). *Dancing desires: Choreographing sexualities on and off the stage.* Madison, WI: University of Wisconsin Press.

Dewey, J. (2007). *Experience and education.* Toronto, ON: Simon and Schuster Canada.

Eisner, E.W. (1991). *The enlightened eye: Qualitative inquiry and the enhancement of educational practice.* New York, NY: Collier Macmillan.

Eisner, E.W. (2002). *The arts and the creation of mind.* New Haven, CT: Yale University Press.

Flintoff, A. (1991). Dance, masculinity and teacher education. *British Journal of Physical Education, 22*(4), 31–5.

Flores, R. (1995). Dance for health: Improving fitness in African American and Hispanic adolescents. *Public Health Reports, 110*(2), 189–93.

Foregger, N., & Miller, D. (1975). Experiments in the art of the dance. *The Drama Review, 19*(1), 74–7. http://dx.doi.org/10.2307/1144971

Foulkes, J.L. (2001). Dance is for American men: Ted Shawn and the intersection of gender, sexuality, and nationalism in the 1930s. In J.C. Desmond (Ed.), *Dancing desires: Choreographing sexualities on and off the stage* (121–39). Madison, WI: University of Wisconsin Press.

Friedlander, L. (Director). (2006, 7 April). *Take the Lead* [Motion picture]. United States: New Line Cinema.

Gallagher, K. (2006). Sexual fundamentalism and performances of masculinity: An ethnographic scene study. *Journal of Gay & Lesbian Issues in Education, 4*(1), 47–76. http://dx.doi.org/10.1300/J367v04n01_05

Gard, M. (2001). Dancing around the "problem" of boys and dance. *Discourse (Abingdon), 22*(2), 213–25. http://dx.doi.org/10.1080/01596300120072383

Gard, M. (2003a). Being someone else: Using dance in anti-oppressive teaching. *Educational Review, 55*(2), 211–23. http://dx.doi.org/10.1080/0013191032000072236

Gard, M. (2003b). Moving and belonging: Dance, sport and sexuality. *Sex Education, 3*(2), 105–18. http://dx.doi.org/10.1080/14681810309037

Gard, M. (2006). *Men who dance: Aesthetics, athletics & the art of masculinity.* New York, NY: Peter Lang.

Gard, M. (2008). When a boy's gotta dance: New masculinities, old pleasures. *Sport Education and Society, 13*(2), 181–93. http://dx.doi.org/10.1080/13573320801957087

Gard, M., & Meyenn, R. (2000). Boys, bodies, pleasure and pain: Interrogating contact sports in schools. *Sport Education and Society, 5*(1), 19–34. http://dx.doi.org/10.1080/135733200114415

Gilbert, G.A. (2003). The male myth. *Dance Teacher, 25*(2), 72–6.

Glaister, I. (1987). Dance education 1938–1958. *British Journal of Physical Education, 18*(3), 104–6.

Grady, J. (2002). *A qualitative study of adult development and career transition in gay male dancers* (Doctoral dissertation). City University of New York. Retrieved from http://search.proquest.com/docview/252085398/fulltextPDF

Griffin, S. (1995). *The eros of everyday life: Essays on ecology, gender and society.* New York: Doubleday.

Grossman, D. (2007). Danny Grossman dance company. Retrieved from http://www.dannygrossman.com

Grosz, E. (1995). *Space, time, and perversion.* London, UK: Routledge.

Hanna, J.L. (1989). Dance education in the public schools. *Dance Teacher Now, 11*(2), 25–32.

Hargreaves, J., & Anderson, E. (2014). *Routledge Handbook of Sport, Gender and Sexuality.* Oxon, UK: Routledge.

Hooks, B. (1994). *Teaching to transgress: Education as the practice of freedom.* London, UK: Routledge.

House, C. (2008). House, Christopher. Retrieved from http://www.tdt.org/about/company/christopher-house/

Howard, R. (2004, January). Without dance, they'd just be … Roni Mahler brings ballet to the sports world. *Dance Magazine.*

Hua, K. (2000, 6 May). His dance touches every single audience's heart, Li is, undoubtedly, the millennium dancer of the year. *Singtao Daily*, p. E3.

Jeyasingh, S. (n.d.). *Jeyasingh Shobana Dance.* Retrieved from http://www.shobanajeyasingh.co.uk/

Kelder, S.H., Perry, C.L., & Klepp, K. (1993). Community-wide youth exercise promotion: Long-term outcomes of the Minnesota heart health program and the class of 1989 study. *Journal of School Health, 63*(5), 218–23.

Kendall, D.E. (2005). *Sociology in our times*. Belmont, CA: Thomson Wadsworth.

Keyworth, S.A. (2001). Critical autobiography: "Straightening" out dance education. *Research in Dance Education, 2*(2), 117–37. http://dx.doi.org/10.1080/14647890120100764

Kidd, B. (1987). Sports and masculinity. In M. Kaufman (Ed.), *Beyond Patriarchy: Essays by Men on Pleasure, Power, and Change* (250–265). New York, NY: Oxford University Press.

Kirk, D. (1993). *The body, schooling and culture*. Geelong, Australia: Deakin University Press.

Kirk, D. (1998). *Schooling bodies: School practice and public discourse 1880–1950*. Leicester, UK: Leicester University Press.

Kisselgoff, A. (1982, 21 March). Merce Cunningham, the maverick of modern dance. *New York Times*, Arts.

Lever, J. (1978). Sex differences in the complexity of children's play and games. *American Sociological Review, 43*(4), 471–83. http://dx.doi.org/10.2307/2094773

Li, Z. (2007, March). *Gender imbalance: Embodied language through male dancers*. Paper and performance presented at the 7th Annual Dean's Graduate Student Research Conference, Ontario Institute for Studies in Education, University of Toronto.

Lipscomb, B. (1986). The trouble with dance is its name. *Bulletin of Physical Education, 22*, 65–8.

Lloyd, M.L., & West, B.H. (1988). Where are the boys in dance? *JOPERD – Journal of Physical Education, Recreation & Dance, 59*(5), 47–51. http://dx.doi.org/10.1080/07303084.1988.10609755

London District Catholic School Board. (2014). Dance Fest – Primary – Junior – Intermediate. Retrieved from https://www.ldcsb.on.ca/Programs/recreationprogram/dancefestival/Pages/default.aspx

Lorber, J. (1994). *Paradoxes of gender*. New Haven, CT: Yale University Press.

Margolin, I. (2008). Creating movement, creating self: A performative inquiry with girls (Unpublished doctoral thesis). OISE, University of Toronto.

Marques, I.A. (1998). Dance education in/and the postmodern. In S.B. Shapiro (Ed.), *Dance, power and difference* (171–185). Champaign, IL: Human Kinetics.

Martino, W. (1999). "Cool boys," "party animals," "squids" and "poofters": Interrogating the dynamics and politics of adolescent masculinities in school. *British Journal of Sociology of Education, 20*(2), 239–63. http://dx.doi.org/10.1080/01425699995434

Maslow, A.H. (1943). A theory of human motivation. *Psychological Review, 50*(4), 370–96. http://dx.doi.org/10.1037/h0054346

McLaren, P. (1999). *Schooling as a ritual performance: Towards a political economy of educational symbols and gestures.* Lanham, MD: Rowman & Littlefield.

Meglin, J.A. (1994). Gender issues in dance education. *JOPERD – Journal of Physical Education, Recreation & Dance, 65*(2), 25–7. http://dx.doi.org/10.1080/07303084.1994.10606850

Messner, M.A. (1999). Becoming 100 percent straight. In J. Coakley & P. Donnelly (Eds.), *Inside Sports* (104–110). London, UK: Routledge.

Messner, M. (1990). Boyhood, organized sports, and the construction of masculinities. *Journal of Contemporary Ethnography, 18*(4), 416–444. http://dx.doi.org/10.1177/089124190018004003

The National Ballet of Canada. (2015). Kudelka, James. Retrieved from https://national.ballet.ca/Meet/Creative-Team/James-Kudelka?

Milner, C. (2002, 13 April). More boys and girls join in the royal ballet. *Telegraph UK.* Retrieved from http://www.telegraph.co.uk/news/1390792/More-boys-than-girls-join-the-Royal-Ballet.html

Minuchin, S., Montalvo, B., Guerney, B.G., Rusman, B., & Schumer, F. (1967). *The families of the slums: An exploration of their structure and treatment.* New York, NY: Basic Books.

Mirault, D. (2000). The boys are back in town: How to bring more boys into your dance class, and keep them there. *Dance Teacher, 5*(1), 11–13.

O'Donnell, C. (1984). *The basis of the bargain: Gender, schooling and jobs.* Crows Nest, Australia: Allen & Unwin.

Olander, M.V. (2007). Painting the voice: Weblogs and writing instruction in the high school classroom (Doctoral dissertation). Nova Southeastern University. Retrieved from http://search.proquest.com/docview/304718270/fulltextPDF

Ontario Institute for Studies in Education of the University of Toronto. (2014). OISE strategic plan 2011–2015: Opening doors in and through education. Retrieved from http://www.oise.utoronto.ca/oise/UserFiles/File/OISE%20STRATEGIC%20PLAN%202011-2015.pdf

Ou, J. (1995, November). Zihao Li is a rising star in dance community. *Beijing Youth Daily*, p. D6.

Palen, L.-A. (2008). Free-time activities and substance use among adolescents in Cape Town, South Africa (Doctoral dissertation). Pennsylvania State University. Retrieved from http://redirect.proquest.com/r?&url=http://proquest.umi.com/pqdweb?did=1633773951&Fmt=7&clientId=12520&RQT=309&VName=PQD

Phelan, P. (1993). *Unmarked: The politics of performances*. London, UK: Burns & Oates. http://dx.doi.org/10.4324/9780203359433

Powell, K.E., Thompson, P.D., Caspersen, C.J., & Kendrick, J.S. (1987). Physical activity and the incidence of coronary heart disease. *Annual Review of Public Health, 8*(1), 253–87. http://dx.doi.org/10.1146/annurev. pu.08.050187.001345

Queen Victoria Public School. (2014). Facts and figures. Retrieved from http://www.tdsb.on.ca/Findyour/Schools/FactsAndFigures.aspx?schno=5267

Ripley, M., Anderson, E., McCormack, M., & Rockett, B. (2012). Heteronormativity in the university classroom: Novelty attachment and content substitution among gay-friendly students. *Sociology of Education, 85*(2), 121–130. http://dx.doi.org/10.1177/0038040711427315

Risner, D. (2008). When boys dance: Cultural resistance in dance education. In S.B. Shapiro (Ed.) *Dance in a World of Change: Examining Globalization and Cultural Differences* (93–115). Champaign, IL: Human Kinetics.

Risner, D. (2009a). Challenges and opportunities for dance pedagogy: Critical social issues and "unlearning" how to teach. Paper presented at the Congress on Research in Dance, De Montfort University, Leicester, UK, June. http://dx.doi.org/10.1017/S2049125500001114

Risner, D. (2009b). When boys dance: Moving masculinities and cultural resistance in dance training and education. Paper presented at the Dance and the Child International, Kingston, Jamaica.

Risner, D. (2009c). *Stigma and perseverance in the lives of boys who dance: An empirical study of male identities in Western theatrical dance training*. Lewiston, NY: Edwin Mellen.

Roenigk, A. (2003). "Where the boys are." *Dance Teacher*. Dance Media LLC, dba Macfadden Performing Arts Media, LLC. https://www.highbeam.com/doc/1P3-289227501.html

Roundell, T. (2002). Arts education in the Pacific region: Heritage and creativity. Paper presented at the Regional Conference on Arts Education, Nadi, Fiji, November.

Sallis, J., McKenzie, T.L., Alcaraz, J.E., Kolody, B., Faucette, N., & Hovell, M.F. (1997). The effects of a 2-year physical education program (SPARK) on physical activity and fitness in elementary school students. sports, play and active recreation for kids. *American Journal of Public Health, 87*(8), 1328–34. http://dx.doi.org/10.2105/AJPH.87.8.1328

Schmitz, N.B. (1990). Key education issues critical to dance education. *JOPERD – Journal of Physical Education, Recreation & Dance, 61*(5), 59–61. http://dx.doi.org/10.1080/07303084.1990.10604518

Schwartz, L.L. (1977). Born curious (Book). *Journal of Personality Assessment,*
   41(4), 438–9. http://dx.doi.org/10.1207/s15327752jpa4104_21

Scraton, S. (1986) Images of femininity and the teaching of girls' physical education. In J. Evans (Ed.), *Physical Education, Sport and Schooling: Studies in the*
   Sociology of Physical Education (71–94). Lewes, UK: Falmer Press.

Seham, J. (1997). The effects on at-risk children of an in-school dance program
   (Unpublished doctoral dissertation). Adelphi University, Garden City, NY.

Shawn, T. (1960). *One thousand and one night stands.* New York, NY: Doubleday
   Publishing.

Siann, G. (2013). *Gender, sex, and sexuality: Contemporary psychological perspectives.*
   London, UK: Taylor & Francis.

Simons-Morton, B.G., Taylor, W.C., Snider, S.A., & Huang, I.W. (1993). The
   physical activity of fifth-grade students during physical education classes.
   American Journal of Public Health, 83(2), 262–264. http://dx.doi.org/10.2105/
   AJPH.83.2.262

Stevens, S. (1992). Dance in the national curriculum. In N. Armstrong (Ed.),
   New Directions in Physical Education (141–54). Champaign, IL: Human Kinetics.

Stinson, S. (1991). Reflections on teacher education in dance. *Design for Arts in*
   Education, 92(3), 23–30. http://dx.doi.org/10.1080/07320973.1991.9935580

Stinson, S., Blumenfield-Jones, D., & van Dyke, J. (1990). Voices of young women
   dance students: An interpretive study of meaning in dance. *Dance Research*
   Journal, 22(2), 13–22. http://dx.doi.org/10.2307/1477780

Stubley, E. (1995). The performer, the score, the work: Musical performance
   and transactional reading. *Journal of Aesthetic Education, 29*(3), 55–69.

Talbot, M. (1993). Physical education and the national curriculum: Some politi-
   cal issues. In G. McFee & A. Tomlinson (Eds.). *Education, sport, and leisure:*
   Connections and controversies (34–64). Brighton, UK: University of Brighton
   Chelsea School Research Centre.

Toronto District School Board. (2009a). Dance programs. Retrieved from
   http://www.tdsb.on.ca/_site/ViewItem.asp?siteid=11&menuid=
   2490&pageid=1985

Toronto District School Board. (2009b). School profile – Rosedale Heights
   School of the Arts. Retrieved from http://www.tdsb.on.ca/profiles/5630.pdf

Toronto District School Board. (2014). Dare2Create Arts Festival 2014.
   Retrieved from http://tdsb.on.ca/News/ArticleDetails/TabId/116/ArtMID/
   474/default.aspx?ArticleID=552

Toronto District School Board. (2016). *About us.* Retrieved from http://tdsb
   .on.ca/AboutUs.aspx

Trent, M. (2008). Artistic director. Retrieved from http://www.dancemakers
   .org/aboutDirector.html

Warner, M.J. (2010). *Dance companies in Toronto.* Toronto, ON: Dance Collection Danse.

Weissberg, R.P., Caplan, M., & Harwood, R.L. (1991). Promoting competent young people in competence-enhancing environments: A systems-based perspective on primary prevention. *Journal of Consulting and Clinical Psychology, 59*(6), 830–41. http://dx.doi.org/10.1037/0022-006X.59.6.830

Williams, C. (1995). *Still a man's world: Men who do women's work.* Berkeley, CA: University of California Press.

Willis, P.E. (1981). *Learning to labor: How working class kids get working class jobs.* New York, NY: Columbia University Press.

Winterson, J. (1995). *Art objects: Essays on ecstasy and effrontery.* New York, NY: Alfred A. Knopf.

York University. (2016). The York Dance Ensemble. Retrieved from http://dance.ampd.yorku.ca/about/performance/york-dance-ensemble/

Yue, X. (2000, 22 May). An exciting moment in dance. *Da Gong Bao,* p. B6.

Zhao, C. (1997, 29 August). After ferocious competition, Zihao is the finalist to receive the prestigious scholarship from the American dance festival to study at the Hong Kong Academy for Performing Arts. *Guangzhou Daily,* p. 15.

Index

Page numbers in italics refer to figures and tables.

Aalten, Anna, 105
Acocella, Joan Ross, 110
Adler, A.H.W., 27–9
adolescent males in dance, 40–54;
    and invisible barriers, 105–19;
    transformation of, 75–104; voices
    of, 55–74. *See also* male dance
    students; males in dance
Ailey, Alvin, 5, 5n4, 7, 81
all-boys dance class. *See under* dance
    classes
Anderson, Eric, 24
Australia, 26, 39, 115

Balanchine, George, 5n3, 23, 69
ballet, 5–6, 11, 23, 31, 39, 42, 46–7,
    63, 66–7, 72, 81, 85–6, 92, 94, 99–
    101, 103, 106–13, 119, 126–7, *129*,
    131, 133–5, 139, 156–7, 159, 162;
    and adolescent boys, 58; classical,
    14; males in, 56; Russian Vaganova,
    14, 14n2; swimming pool, 148–9;
    use in sports, 62
Ballet Jörgen, 156
Barone, Tom, 56
Baryshnikov, Mikhail, 7, 9–10, 23, 65,
    117

Benoit, Mary, 88
Berger, Amanda J., 26, 88
Bev, Day, 88
bisexuality, 23, 25. *See also* males in
    dance
Bleakley, E.W., 36, 100
Blount, Jackie, 109
Blumenfield-Jones, D., 71
Bond, Karen, 39, 88
Booth, David, 25
boys in dance. *See* adolescent males
    in dance; male dance students
Brennan, Deirdre, 36, 38, 85, 88, 100;
    *Dance in the Northern Ireland Physical
    Education Curriculum*, 87
Britain's Got Talent, 115
Burt, Ramsay, 46; *Alien Bodies*, 4;
    The Male Dancer, 4, 30

Canada Council for the Arts, 157,
    159
Canada's National Ballet School, 40,
    45–7, 72, 123, 135, 156, 159
Carroll, Thomas, 51
China, 10, *13*, 14, 18, 23, 28, 43,
    45, 63, 114–15, 149–50; People's
    Liberation Army (PLA), 12, 14.

See also Li, Zihao; Qian Jin Dance Company
Cole, Ardra, 56
Collective of Black Artists (COBA), 131
Connell, Robert, 110
Cook, Matt, 62
Crawford, John, 88
Csikszentmihalyi, Mihaly, 19
Cuba, 114; dancers from, 156
Cunningham, Merce, 5n3, 81–2, 103

D'Amboise, Jacques, 69
dance and physical education, 7, 27–8, 32–3, 35–8, 58, 78–9, 87, 95, 99–100, 109–10, 114, 161–2
dance classes: all-boys, 41–4, 50–1, *53*, 55–7, 60, 63, 69, 74, 79, 82–3, 85, 87, 97, 105–6, 123–6, 128, *130*, 131, 133–6, *138–40*, 148, 159, 161; mixed-gender, 38, 41, *44*, 51, *53*, 55, 63, 85, 87, 123, 128, 131, *132*, 134, 136, 148. *See also* male dance students
dance curriculum, 31–5, 148, 156
dance education: promotion of, and initiatives, 152–62; teaching strategies, 8, 38–9, 85, 148–9; use of video in, 23, 56, 114–15, 117, 148
dance performances in schools, 155–8, 160–1. *See also under* male dance students
dance training: formal/professional, 5; informal/recreational/educational, 5, 43, 48, 58; pre-professional/ career preparation, 5, 6–7, 40, 43, 45–7, 114, *124*, 155n1. *See also* dance and physical education; dance education

Dancer & Me assignment, 50, 55–74
Dancing with the Stars, 3, 7, 92
David Suzuki Secondary School, 158
DeMarco, T., 79
Desiraeda Dance Theatre, 15, *20*
Desmond, Jane, 7
Dewey, John, 51, 92; *Experience and Education*, 26

Earl Haig Secondary School, 40, 97, 157
Eisner, Elliot, 56; *The Arts and the Creation of Mind*, 52
England, 6, 115
ethnic dance, 3, 46, 108, 159–61
ethnicity, and adolescent males in dance, 43–7
Etobicoke School of the Arts (ESA), 34, 40, 45, 96–7

family, importance of support from, 7, 48–9, 69, 83, 89–92, 94, 98–9, 104
Flintoff, Anne, 28, 109–10
flow, 19, 136, 146–7, 162
Foulkes, J.L., 37

Gallagher, Kathleen, 24
"Gangnam Style" (Psy), 3, 117
Gard, Michael, 7, 27, 29, 36–7, 39, 88, 95, 100, 105–6, 110, 122; *Men Who Dance*, 4–5
gender and masculinity, 24–5. *See also* masculinity/masculinization
gender imbalance, 5, 29, 34, 37, 49, 100, 136
Glaister, Irene, 36, 100
Grady, Joseph, 88
Graham, Martha, 5n3
Griffin, Susan, 8, 27

Grossman, Danny, 30
Grosz, Elizabeth: *Space, Time, and Perversion*, 75

Hanna, Judith Lynne, 86
Hargreaves, Jennifer, 24
heterosexuality, 8, 27, 29, 58. *See also* males in dance
hip hop, 3, 6, 39, 66, 80–1, 95, 109, 111, 119, 157, 159–61
homosexuality, 8, 25, 27–9, 38, 58, 109–10. *See also* males in dance
Hong Kong Academy for Performing Arts, 5–6, 15
House, Christopher, 30
Howard, Rachel, 62

identity, 7, 15, 24–7, 29, 31, 53–4, 56, 96, 98, 122; racial, 110. *See also* masculinity/masculinization

jazz, 31, 38–9, 42, 56, 66, 113, 126, 134, 157
Jeyasingh, Shobana, 73

Kaeja d'Dance, 156
Kelly, Gene, 7, 117
Keyworth, S.A., 37
Kidd, Bruce, 62
Knowles, Gary, 56
krump, 3, 6, 32, 80, 135, 160
Kudelka, James, 30

Lever, J., 27
Li, Zihao, and history in dance, 9–24, 149–50
Limón, José, 5, 5n2
Lipscomb, B., 26, 38; "The Trouble with Dance Is Its Name," 71

Lloyd, M.L., 36
London District Catholic School Board, 158
Lorber, Judith, 26

Mahler, Roni, 62
male dance students: dance performances, 52–4, 60, 69, 91–2, 94, 96, 104, 113, *135*, 137–46; experience of dance class, 123–36; first dance experience, 120–3; show time, 137–46
male dance teachers, 6–8, 23, 26, 29–30, 37–41, 75, 85, 87–9, 104, 112, 130, 159
males in dance, 4–7; being labelled "gay," 24, 27, 29, 55, 58, 98, 109, 116, 130; pressures and challenges, 147; stereotypes about, 37, 105, 109–12, 114, 116–19, 144, 152. *See also* bisexuality; heterosexuality; homosexuality; male dance students
Margolin, I., 35
Marques, I.A., 37
Martha Graham Company, 5n3, 82
Martino, Wayne, 28, 38
masculinity/masculinization, 4, 18, 22–5, 27–9, 37, 65, 110, 122
Maslow, Abraham, 144
media and technology, 7, 22–3, 25, 51–2, 65, 89, 104, 111, 114–17, 116, 121, 123, 127, 135, 137, 148, 153; *Britain's Got Talent*, 115; *Dancing with the Stars*, 3, 7, 92; *So You Think You Can Dance*, 3, 7, 22–3, 50, 65, 89, 92–3, 112, 115–17; YouTube, 7, 50, 115, 117, 148, 163

Meglin, Joellen, 110
Messner, Michael, 62
Meyenn, Robert, 29, 105–6
Mirault, Don, 37, 87
mixed-gender dance classes. *See under* dance classes
modern dance, 5–6, 23, 27, 29, 31, 42, 46, 56, 66–7, 85, 106, 109, 113, 126, 131, 133, 155

New York, 104, 112; dance in public schools, 35, 40–1; Juilliard School, 93
New York City Ballet, 69, 92
Nureyev, Rudolf, 23, 65

O'Donnell, Carol: *The Basis of the Bargain*, 109
Olander, Marilyn, 51
Ontario artist-in-residence programs, 32
Ontario Arts Council, 157
Ontario arts curriculum, 31–5, 50, 148, 158
Ontario Institute for Studies in Education (OISE), 156
Opera Atelier, 15, 86, 102, 112, 123, 127, 131, 156–7

Palen, Lori-Ann, 28
Phelan, Peggy, 53
physical education curriculum, 32–3, 35–6, 100, 158. *See also* dance and physical education
Pulse Ontario Youth Dance Conference, 31
Pynkoski, Marshall, 86, 123

Qian Jin Dance Company, 12, *13*, 22
Queen Victoria Public School, 160

religion and dance: First Nations, 3; Tibetan, 3, 46
Risner, Doug, 27, 76, 104, 145; *Stigma and Perseverance in the Lives of Boys Who Dance*, 6–7
Rosedale Heights School of the Arts (RHSA), 3–4, 23, 33–4, 41, 62–3, 65–6, 68, 76, 78, 81–3, 89–90, 94, 102–3, 105, 108, 118, 121, 136, 147–50, 158; choreographic workshop, 137–8; hip hop club, 80, 160; males in dance program, 40–2, 47, 55, 58, 85–7, 97–9, 111, 123–30
Russia, 10, 14, 23, 108, 114

Sallis, James, 62
Schmitz, N.B., 35
Schwartz, Lita Linzer, 71
Scraton, S., 172
Seham, Jenny, 69, 76
Shawn, Ted, 27, 27n1, 29, 46, 58, 93
Sidney, K., 79
So You Think You Can Dance, 3, 7, 22–3, 50, 65, 89, 92–3, 112, 115–17
Spain, 39
sports, 27–8, 36, 58, 62, 79, 92, 95, 99–100, 110, 150–1
Stevens, Sarah, 36, 100
Stinson, S.W., 34, 39, 71
Stubley, Eleanor: *The Performer, the Score, the Work*, 146

Talbot, Margaret, 37, 87–8
tap, 31, 83
Taylor, Paul, 5, 5n3
television shows. *See names of individual shows*
Toronto, 15, 30, 34–5, 97, 108; pre-professional training facilities, gender representation in, 45–6

Toronto Arts Council, 159
Toronto Dance Theatre (TDT), 40, 46, 50, 156–7
Toronto District School Board, 6, 40–1, 153; performing arts and dance initiatives, 158–60
Trent, Michael, 30

United States, 5nn3–4, 6n5, 10, 39–41, 46, 69, 71, 102, 115
University of Macau, 9, 28
University of Toronto, 156

Van Dyke, J., 71
video documentary, 163–4

West, B.H., 36
Williams, Christine, 26; *Still a Man's World*, 122
Winterson, Jeanette, 8

York Dance Ensemble (YDE), 155, 155n1
York University, 6, 31n7, 40; dance program, 154–6
YouTube, 7, 50, 115, 117, 148, 163

Lightning Source UK Ltd.
Milton Keynes UK
UKOW04f0413071117
312317UK00001B/73/P